The JOYS of CRISIS

The JOYS of CRISIS

How U.S. AWASTHI Scripted the Rise of IFFCO

AARNAB MITRA

RUPA

Published by
Rupa Publications India Pvt. Ltd 2023
7/16, Ansari Road, Daryaganj
New Delhi 110002

Sales Centres:
Prayagraj Bengaluru Chennai
Hyderabad Jaipur Kathmandu
Kolkata Mumbai

Photographs courtesy: IFFCO archives and the personal collection of U.S. Awasthi

P-ISBN: 978-93-5702-236-1
E-ISBN: 978-93-5702-229-3

First impression 2023

10 9 8 7 6 5 4 3 2 1

Printed in India

CONTENTS

ONE

FROM SATHANI TO BENARES

The war in Europe had ended two months ago, on 8 May 1945, and Japan was only a couple of months away from capitulating. The world was breathing a little easier. But India was in ferment. The end of the Second World War and the visible weakening of British power had raised hopes of independence coming early. Nationalistic fervour was running high. An ancient land, forced into stupor for a thousand years, was getting ready to awaken again. The atmosphere in India's cities, towns, villages and countryside was charged.

Udai Shanker Awasthi was born in this electric milieu on 12 July 1945, in Sathani, a nondescript village in Uttar Pradesh's Unnao district. It was the norm in those days, especially among wealthy families, for women to bear children in their natal homes and return to their husband's house months after the birth of their child.

Durgavati Awasthi, nee Pandey, who came from a highly respected and wealthy family who owned large tracts of agricultural land and ran a successful business, broke with the norms and decided to stay back in her marital home for the birth of her fifth child, Udai Shanker. This was surprising as she was the only daughter in the Pandey family. She had two brothers who were older than her. Though they were not zamindars (feudal lords), the Pandeys were rich enough and wielded lots of influence in the area. Their great-grandfathers had been soldiers in the army of Rana Beni Madho, the leader of Baiswara in the First War of Independence in 1857. When the British government started executing people for their participation in the war, the Pandeys fled to Calcutta (now Kolkata) to save their lives, settled there and started a business.

The Awasthi family, though not as affluent as the Pandeys, also had a business—in Pachoda, near Nashik in Maharashtra—in the garments trade. Their great-grandfather was a subedar in the British Army. He had fought in Afghanistan in the First World War and was as famous as Subedar Baba. In those days, 'subedar' was the highest rank open to Indians from non-aristocratic families.

Father's early death

The Awasthis were a large family even by the standards of Indian joint families. Awasthi's father, Shiv Madho, was the fourth among five brothers. He kept shifting between farming and business and travelled a lot for work—sometimes to Pachoda in Maharashtra and sometimes to Bengal. Given his peripatetic existence, it was more convenient for Durgavati to stay with her children in her maternal home in Poorey Pandey, about 25 kilometres from Sathani.

Shiv Madho was a very self-respecting man who did not give in to anyone. He ran a business in Nashik for some years and then moved to Calcutta. There he tried his hand at a business but that, too, did not last long. Thereafter, he shifted to Kanpur and did some odd jobs before returning to his native village, where he took up farming.

'He was not very successful. Perhaps, he was too idealistic,' said Rekha, Awasthi's younger sister. Shiv Madho died on 13 August 1947 when Awasthi was a child and Rekha a toddler.

Growing up in an atmosphere of patriotism

The Awasthi and Pandey families were both actively involved in the freedom struggle. One of Awasthi's uncles from his father's side was a gram pradhan, and later became a corporator in Kanpur. In British India and in the early years of independence, being a corporator was a matter of pride and status.

As was the norm in those days, most family members wore khadi. Durgavati used to spin yarn on the charkha, and her children wore clothes made up of those yarns. 'I opened my eyes in a world charged with extreme pride and love for the country. There was tremendous love for one's mother tongue. People took extreme pride in their culture. Everyone wore khadi. I grew up in that atmosphere,' said Awasthi, adding that that is why he loves India so passionately.

Durgavati's second brother, Kedar Nath Pandey, was in politics. He was associated with the socialist wing of the Congress, under Narendra Dev. Renowned historian Bipan Chandra's book, *India's Struggle for Independence*, describes Kedar Nath's contribution to the freedom struggle and even carries a photograph of him and his wife. Kedar Nath, a contemporary of Jayaprakash Narayan, was jailed for his involvement in the freedom struggle. He stayed in prison with Jawaharlal Nehru.

The freedom movement had sparked awareness about women's education. The wife of Uma Shanker Pandey, Durgavati's eldest brother, was a well-educated lady. She was very fond of Durgavati and encouraged her to read *Kalyan* and *Saraswati*, two leading Hindi literary magazines of that era. This inculcated in Durgavati a lifelong passion for education and knowledge, which she took pains to instil in her children. Every morning, she would embrace her children and make them say a prayer to Goddess Saraswati, the goddess of knowledge.

She was also very fond of reciting the Ramayana and listening to it being recited. Awasthi would read the epic to his mother whenever she felt sad, and this would lift her spirits immediately.

Admission in two schools

Given her unsettled circumstances—sometimes living in Sathani and at other times in Poorey Pandey—it was, perhaps, natural that her children were admitted to schools in both villages. 'We sat in a bullock cart in the morning and reached Poorey Pandey by evening. We would study in both the villages,' Awasthi recalls.

As an indication of the family's influence, the school at Poorey Pandey was started for the benefit of the Awasthi children. This naturally benefited the entire village.

'Those days, things were not as structured as they are now. The boy who used to carry my inkpot and books—he also studied with us—became a sarpanch [head of the village]. The boy who used to accompany me in Sathani also became a sarpanch,' Awasthi said, with a twinkle in his eyes.

Undisputed leader of his group

There were few restrictions in Poorey Pandey, and little Rekha followed Awasthi wherever he went. It wasn't just her. Almost every other boy his age would follow him everywhere. 'He had a big group of friends, both in Poorey Pandey and Sathani,' she said. 'He was the undisputed leader of both the groups. We had a jeep in Poorey Pandey. Sudhir Bhai's [Awasthi's nickname] favourite sport was rolling discarded tyres of the jeep with a stick. They would often play Chor Police, and he would invariably be the police.' She laughs.

Awasthi was a brave child. 'He did not fear snakes or scorpions. He would immediately take a torch, call the servants and go looking for them. The whole day he would keep asking me to go away from him, but when evening came, he would say: "Rekha, come with me," because the only thing he feared was darkness.'

He was also very fond of cricket and played without pads and gloves. 'He would go out every morning to play cricket with his friends,' remembers his sister.

'I think those early blows hardened me for the life ahead,' Awasthi said with a smile.

Those days also taught him to treat everyone equally and fairly, irrespective of caste, religion or status. The woman who cleaned their toilets, who was considered an untouchable, would finish her work and chat with his mother through the afternoon. He would sometimes visit her house while playing in the village. Many of his friends, with whom he spent most of his free time, belonged to the so-called lower castes. Nobody ever tried to stop him from interacting with them or treating them with respect, except once. Many decades later, in 2013 or 2014, Awasthi had organized a feast in his village and invited everyone. As he sat down for the meal with his friends, a cousin tried to dissuade him, citing the difference in their caste status. Awasthi simply told him to mind his own business and carried on eating his meal in the company of those he had grown up with. Awasthi said it was Mahatma Gandhi's sermons against untouchability that gave his family this progressive outlook.

Taking command

Awasthi began to display leadership traits from a very early age. The Pandey house was inside a gated campus, and had an elevated front verandah. Awasthi, then barely six or seven years old, would take the attendance of ten to twelve farm hands who worked on the family's fields. The workers, all adults and almost double his size, thought nothing about submitting to his authority.

Little Awasthi was then the only male member of the family present at the Pandey house. His eldest mama, Uma Shanker, was away looking after his iron business in Kanpur while Kedar Nath was busy with politics, which he pursued from the nearby town of Lalganj. Awasthi's older brother, Devi Shanker, and his cousin were away for higher studies. So, perforce, he had to take charge.

Awasthi combined his still-nascent leadership qualities with discipline and a sharp focus on his goals. 'He was 10–11 years old. I remember him as a very focused child. He had his time slots for studies, for playing and for other activities. On particular days each week, he would do community service, like sweeping the locality and cleaning the drains. He was a happy child, but he was not careless. He was rational and intelligent,' said Kamlesh Awasthi, who married Devi Shanker in 1956.

Awasthi remains very fond of Kamlesh to this day and makes it a point to touch her feet and seek her blessings whenever he visits her in Kanpur.

Moving to Kanpur

The family moved to Kanpur when Dr Devi Shanker Awasthi got a job as a lecturer in DAV College in 1953. Awasthi had just passed Class 5; Rekha was in Class 2.

'We moved to Kanpur for better education,' Awasthi said.

It was a huge change from his life in the village. 'Kanpur was like a dream for us—electricity, metal roads, water from taps, big shops, hotels and restaurants, cars, trains and cinema…It had everything that we had heard about and imagined.' Rekha chuckles.

The family lived on the first and second floors of a house that had shops on the ground floor, in an area called Maniram Bagiya. The locality was a wholesale market for stationery items. There were some printing presses there as well.

Awasthi and Rekha shared a room. There were two tables in the room but, as children are wont to, they often fought over who would sit at the table near the window.

'Sudhir Bhai woke very early, at 4.00 a.m., every morning. He would study and then go to play cricket. I practised the sitar in the morning, and that was his time to study. He used to get very upset with me. But I usually woke an hour after him; so, by the time I picked up my sitar, he would have left for cricket. Yet, there were days when our timings clashed and he would get very angry,' recalls his sister, adding that in Kanpur, as in Poorey Pandey and Sathani, Awasthi had a large group of friends.

There was a charitable trust called Balkan-Ji-Bari for the education and entertainment of children. It was founded by Padma Shri Dada Sevak Bhojraj, a renowned social worker, in 1923. They also took up cleanliness drives in the neighbourhood.

It was here that Awasthi's fetish for cleanliness became evident. As the leader of the group in Balkan-Ji-Bari, he would organize children to clean the drains of the area. They would sweep the road, clean the drains and put lime in them. They would do this every week, and then go to play cricket or badminton. From there they would return home, bathe, eat breakfast and go to school—walking and running for the most part. Awasthi spent most of his evenings at the trust's office, which had a small library.

'I have zero tolerance for dirt and disorder. I always keep things tidy and in perfect order. I have had a structured lifestyle from the very beginning. I did everything myself with my own hands and never depended on anyone else to do anything for me,' he said.

'We never thought about the caste and religion of the people we met or worked with. That has been my mental make-up from my early days; even today, that's how I live my life and do business. I realized the power of caste and experienced casteism first hand only when I took charge of Pyrites Phosphates & Chemicals Limited (PPCL) many decades later,' he said.

In school, too, Awasthi was recognized as the leader. 'Before the morning prayer, I used to speak for five minutes about something related to the country. I had the freedom to choose the topic. My friends used to complain that I waste their five minutes every day.' He guffaws.

Why he became an engineer

Having grown up in a milieu charged with patriotism, it was, thus, natural for Awasthi to nurse a deep desire to do something for the country. In those days, large industries were being hailed as the new 'temples of modern India'. The country was facing an acute shortage of engineers. That was why Awasthi decided to become an engineer and do something for the country.

He wanted to do more for the country. Having grown up in villages, he knew, first hand, the problems and hardships faced by farmers and felt a deep desire to do something to alleviate their lot.

These twin aspirations would, over the next six decades, help transform the lives of millions of farmers across India.

Engineering not politics

After intermediate, Awasthi had to do B.Sc. for one year because he was still a year short of being eligible for admission into any engineering college. At that time, he considered a career in politics. But when he analysed, evaluated and understood the realities of his situation, he realized that if he were to join politics, he would not be able to do what he wanted to do for the country. If, in contrast, he became a competent engineer and did good work in his profession, he would be able to serve the country better.

In 1961, he decided against joining politics. He would remain a student of politics but would shy away from active involvement. He, however, wanted to be able to impact politics wherever possible.

'That's why I have friends across all the political parties. I express my views frankly before them about what is good, what is bad and what will not be in the interest of the country. People listen to me because they know I am not in politics. The government has adopted many programmes of the Indian Farmers Fertiliser Cooperative Limited (IFFCO). The present regime adopted some. The previous regime had also adopted some,' he said.

For example, the Uttar Pradesh government implemented direct benefit transfer (DBT) in seeds, which Awasthi had been asking them to do for a long time. 'So,' he adds with a look of satisfaction, 'I have been able to influence politics in some ways. I have not done it directly; I have done it indirectly, from behind the scenes, but I have made my contribution.'

Admission into BHU

His choice to study engineering over going into politics took him to Banaras Hindu University (BHU). The fees, hostel deposit and other charges were ₹500, which was sent to the university by money order. Armed with the postal receipt, he got on a train from Kanpur and reached Benares after five or six hours. Once there, he took a rickshaw and reached BHU.

He was allotted a room with double occupancy and shown the canteen and mess. 'My first few days at BHU were terrible. I had studied in a Hindi medium school all my life, and knew little English. The classes and the books were all in English; so, the teaching went over my head,' he said with disarming candour.

His outfit—khadi kurta-pyjama—also made him stand out in the crowd like a sore thumb. 'Most of those from my peer group were from rich urban families, children of senior officers in the government and the private sector, or scions of business families. Initially, I felt like a duck out of water,' recalls Awasthi.

Some seniors decided to rag him. But very soon, they became his friends.

'How much money do you have on you?' they asked.

He had about ₹100, a very decent sum of money in those days.

The seniors took ₹30 from him. They then bought him two shirts and two pairs of trousers. They made him subscribe to *The Times of India* and told him to read the paper every day. They also took him to watch English films every week.

He is grateful to his seniors for guiding him. 'They seemed hostile initially. But slowly, over a six-month period, I mastered the language and began to understand what was being taught,' he said, adding that he would never have learnt English but for their 'ragging'.

'You can't acquire engineering knowledge without understanding English,' he adds.

Agitation at BHU

In keeping with his resolve, Awasthi stayed away from politics during his student days. There was, however, one incident at BHU where he was directly involved in an agitation. In 1965, the Government of India introduced the Banaras Hindu University Amendment Bill in Parliament to change the name of the university to Madan Mohan Malaviya Kashi Vishwavidyalaya.

M.C. Chagla was the education minister of India and N.H. Bhagwati was the vice chancellor of the university. All of BHU rose against the Bill. Awasthi played an active role in the agitation and was among the students who spearheaded it. The government was forced to withdraw the Bill.

Recounting the events decades later, Awasthi denies any religious bias in his decision to participate in the stir. 'I thought they should have done that [changed the name] in the case of Aligarh Muslim University as well. They should either have left BHU alone or changed the names of both universities. People felt something undesirable was happening…So this was one major agitation at BHU where I was directly involved,' he said.

Awasthi admits he has no idea about what compulsions the then prime minister had while proposing the change. Like many Indians then, he had extremely high regard for Jawaharlal Nehru and for all the leaders who had fought for India's freedom.

'I had as much regard for Lal Bahadur Shastri as I had for Syama Prasad Mookerjee, Maulana Azad and Rafi Ahmad Kidwai. I also greatly admired Subhas Chandra Bose, Chandra Shekhar Azad and Bhagat Singh, and had the greatest regard and love for Mahatma Gandhi,' he adds.

Brother's death

Dr Devi Shanker Awasthi joined Delhi University as a lecturer in Hindi in 1961. Rekha was admitted to the Hindi honours programme at Delhi's Kirori Mal College in 1963. Three years later, Awasthi was in his final year and the future was looking bright for all the Awasthi siblings when disaster struck.

Devi Shanker died in a scooter accident in 1966, at the very young age of thirty-six. He was rapidly gaining recognition as writer and a literary critic. His wife was in her late-twenties and their three children had just started going to school. Out of the blue, the Awasthi family was left facing a bleak future.

Awasthi remembers those days vividly. 'I was doing my engineering programme,' he said. 'It was a calamity for the family. My mother and my bhabhi showed exemplary courage and wisdom in that period of crisis. My mother had lost her precious son; Bhabhi had lost her husband, and the children had lost their father.'

Awasthi was as badly impacted as the other members of his family. All his uncles and members of the Pandey family rallied around them.

'As a result, I did not feel as helpless as the other members of the family. All my uncles in both the families—paternal and maternal—have always been very respectful towards me. No one ever spoke to me in a raised voice. I have been fortunate since childhood that people have always given me what I wanted,' he said, recounting those dark days. 'In the first place, I never ask anyone for anything. That has been my nature. I enjoy giving. I shrink at the idea of asking someone for something. I always tell everyone that I do not have money, but I am never short of money,' he adds wistfully.

Mother, a source of strength

More than half a century later, Devi Shanker's death is still a painful memory for Kamlesh Awasthi. 'We suffer setbacks and come out of them,' she said stoically. 'That's life. We remained benumbed and dazed for years together. No one talked about it. It was such a delicate issue. Sudhir had a year left of his engineering [programme]; my children had barely started going to school. My daughter was a baby still. We all struggled in our own ways. Ammaji [Awasthi's mother] was our source of strength. She was an exceptional lady.'

As her carefully nurtured family faced an existential crisis, Durgavati took charge once again.

'Amma took care of Bhabhi,' said Rekha. 'She held her grief to herself. She had encountered so many deaths in her life [...] she had lost two daughters earlier. Then she lost her husband. And then this tragedy [Devi Shanker's death] shattered the whole family. But Amma and Bhabhi fought an exemplary battle and kept the family on course.'

Durgavati's courage and fortitude in the face of grave personal tragedy was matched at every step by Kamlesh Awasthi's pluck. Refusing to get cowed down by her circumstances, she got a job as a teacher in the school her children were studying in. A year later, Awasthi finished his engineering degree and joined Shriram Fertilizers in Kota. Then, Kamlesh Awasthi became a lecturer in a college in Kanpur.

The family had survived the trauma of death and was back on track mainly because of Durgavati's influence.

'Today Sudhir Bhai is at the peak of his career, but there is a great struggle behind it. He has made many personal sacrifices to keep the whole family bound together. We, brothers and sisters, our children, and the larger Awasthi and the Pandey families...are connected and are a happy and thriving unit. He is the magnet at the centre of this large circle,' Rekha says of her elder brother.

His mother's genes

Awasthi credits his grit, determination, steadfastness of character and people management skills to his mother's genes.

'She was strong and generous and a woman of intellect. She had a very tough life. She lost her husband at a young age, and then she lost her elder son. My father was in his late forties when he died. People have told me they were extremely attached to each other,' Awasthi says.

Remarkably, especially for a rural woman in that era, Durgavati could read and write. She was self-taught, and had learnt to read and appreciate literature. She also had the ability to take everyone along and was, thus, respected both by her in-laws as well as in her maternal home.

She had good relations with everyone—her husband, her children and their spouses, her brothers and their wives and her neighbours. They listened to her and valued her advice. She lived a frugal life.

'She taught me how to stand firm with dignity in a male-dominated society,' said Kamlesh.

Stories of Durgavati's courage in the face of adversity are legendary in the extended Awasthi clan.

'Amma did not tell me in detail, but I have gathered from older family members that she had to struggle a lot in life. I am the youngest in the family. The oldest among us was our sister Vidya, who was nineteen years older than me. She passed away in 2011. I was born after her marriage. Bhai Sahab [Devi Shanker] came next. He was seventeen years older than me. Two more sisters were born after him, but they did not survive. Amma lost sight in one eye in this period because of wrong medication. Then, after a long gap of fifteen years, Sudhir Bhai and I were born within a few years of each other,' said Rekha.

Passing out as an engineer

The family had still not recovered fully from the shock of Devi Shanker's untimely demise when Awasthi passed out of BHU in 1967 as a chemical engineer. There was a big depression in the market and jobs were scarce.

It was a very difficult time for Awasthi to find a job. He was looking for a vacancy in the fertilizer industry. Awasthi's choice, to join the fertilizer sector, was a direct result of the patriotic spirit he had imbibed in his formative years. 'I felt that I should be in the fertilizer industry because fertilizers could increase agricultural production. I had chosen chemical engineering for this reason. There was an acute food shortage in the country. I had seen the import of wheat from America under the PL-480 programme,' he said.

There was another reason as well: the 1962 war with China, when groups of volunteers began patrolling the BHU campus to guard the water tanks as there was a strong rumour that the enemy might poison the water.

Blackouts were observed. Awasthi actively participated as a volunteer for guarding the campus. But like many Indians, the defeat in the war left him devastated. He had written a few poems in Hindi during that period. One of them read: '*Saintis hazar foot ki oonchai par chade hue saintalis karod log, apne pet ko bajate hain aur chillate hain, jo de uska bhala* ... [Forty-seven crore people standing at a height of thirty-seven thousand feet, clamouring for food, thanking those who give and also those who don't].'

'It hurt me that our country was not prepared to face external aggression. I loved my country so much. I had such pride in my country. I was ashamed that our soldiers did not have proper equipment to fight. Although they fought bravely, we lost. Lata Mangeshkar's song *Ae Mere Watan ke Logon* touched my heart. It still gives me goose bumps when I listen to it,' he said.

But Awasthi did not let that humiliation deflate his spirit. Drawing from his inner reserves of positivity, he promised to help India grow stronger and more powerful, and applied himself to doing whatever good he could for the country.

'Today, I can say that I have tried to make the country self-reliant in fertilizers. If you look at the expansions and the joint ventures (JVs) of IFFCO, you will see what we have done for food security and nutrient security in the country. So, whenever the opportunity came, I did what I thought was right for the country. It was in that spirit that I built the Senegal plant, the plants in Oman and Jordan and the company in Dubai. All these ventures were conceived and set up with the larger objective of making the country self-reliant when it comes to fertilizers,' he said with obvious pride.

The spirit of patriotism and nationalism that had been imbued in him as a child and in his formative years still runs strong. He still gets overwhelmed when he hears Shyamlal Gupta's (Parshad's) song '*Vijayi vishwa tiranga pyara, jhanda uncha rahe hamara*' and Makhanlal Chaturvedi's poem, '*Pushp ki abhilasha*'. 'We published '*Azadi ki agnishikhayen*' to commemorate the fiftieth year of Independence. It was a childhood dream, and I realized it in 1997. There is still that deep desire and strong will to serve the country and do something good for it,' said Awasthi emphatically.

TWO

GOA(L) SETTING

In 1967, when Awasthi graduated from BHU as a chemical engineer, India was still considered a backward third world country. Many of the facilities that students take for granted now weren't available then. For one, there were no campus placements. Fresh graduates were expected to find jobs using their own networks.

Kanpur,. where his family was based, didn't have many jobs for someone as qualified as he. New Delhi was then gaining importance as a commercial and industrial hub. It was also emerging as a magnet for job seekers from far and wide. He was now staying with his family at his deceased brother's residence in Delhi's Model Town.

Awasthi was among the hundreds of thousands of young men who streamed into the national capital to follow a calling. Every morning, he would set out with Re 1 in his pocket to look for a job—25 paise for the ticket for the Delhi Transport Corporation bus service that would allow him unlimited travel for one day, and the remaining, 75 paise, for his meals and any incidental expenses.

One day, he saw a board with the words 'Shriram Fertilizers' in Jhandewalan and walked into their office. He had always wanted to work in the fertilizer sector. The human resources (HR) manager was a man called Mr Chopra. Awasthi parked himself outside his office for three to four hours every day, hoping to get a job.

His persistence finally paid off. Mr Chopra arranged for an interview with the noted industrialist, Charat Ram, the owner of Shriram Fertilizers. After a long and arduous wait, the interview was anti-climactic.

'Why do you want to work in Shriram Fertilizers?' Charat Ram asked him.

'You are setting up a modern plant...that's why,' Awasthi replied.

'How much do you want?

'Whatever you give,' was his short reply.

That was it—he had gotten his dream job. He rushed to Chopra and told the bemused HR manager to give him the appointment letter that very day. His designation: graduate trainee engineer. His salary: ₹450 per month, plus ₹50 scooter allowance. Upon reaching home, he found another appointment letter waiting for him—from the state-owned Fertilizer Corporation of India Ltd., where he had also appeared for an interview. The public sector company was offering him a higher salary of ₹550 per month.

But he had given Mr Chopra his word. So, he decided to accept the offer from Shriram Fertilizers. Everyone at home was happy.

His first job

He boarded the Dehradun Express at night and reached Kota the next morning. There he asked a rickshaw puller where Shriram employees were staying. 'In a shopping complex,' he was told and taken to Rajoria Store, a large general provisions store. The owner, Mr Rajoria, on learning that he had come to join Shriram Fertilizers, showed him a house where a few other executives were staying. It had four to five rooms, one bathroom and a central hall, and each occupant had one room to himself. Rajoria Store provided them with all the provisions. A servant was appointed to cook meals for the residents.

The next day, armed with a bottle of water, he boarded a tempo three-wheeler and proceeded to the site where Shriram Fertilizers was putting up a plant. Work began early at the site. His official working hours were from 7.00 a.m. to 5.00 p.m. Everyone had to punch in to mark attendance.

His first posting was in the urea department, and he was allotted a seat in a tin shed, which had two to three fans. In the summer, it was hot and uncomfortable, but Awasthi and his colleagues—mostly young engineers—didn't mind. The adrenaline rush of building a factory from ground up more than compensated for any physical discomfort.

Awasthi's responsibilities revolved around the project to set up the factory. He had to check all the equipment and their components, check drawings and designs and supervise the construction of the unit he was working on. He rarely left the site at 5.00 p.m., preferring to put in extra hours for the sheer joy of watching the factory take shape before his eyes.

And after work, he and his friends would play bridge, party and enjoy themselves.

At work, he would make it a point to walk around the site with a wrench and a screwdriver and fix any malfunctioning machine himself. 'I never called the maintenance department,' he said with visible pride.

The company was using Dutch technology. Engineers had come from Holland to train the Indian staff on how to set up and run the plant. The operating manual had dozens of pages. There were hundreds of pipes and valves. The Indian engineers were initially trained on simulators. Operations began after that. Awasthi was a quick learner, and he soon mastered the drawings—and could tell exactly what was where and even diagnose problems just by listening to the sound of the machines.

Those early days would stand him in good stead throughout his career. 'I had to go through the grind—setting up and operating plants. So, even today, engineers have to come for discussions fully prepared. I know how machines behave. I know where the valves are. I know the weak points. So, no one can pull wool over my eyes,' said Awasthi.

An important lesson: safety first

In the fertilizer industry, prilling towers play an important role. These towers are tall—about ninety metres—and are cast in concrete. The roof at the Kota plant was being cast; steel scaffolding was holding it in place while the roof was extended and cured, metre by metre.

A Mr Makhijani, an engineer, and a Mr Khanijo, the foreman, were in charge of the work. Probably in order to speed up the work, they decided to extend the roof before the portion cast had been cured.

It was 8.00 p.m. Awasthi, as usual, was working well beyond his scheduled hours. Suddenly, there was a loud rumbling noise, like a bomb exploded. The roof of the prilling tower had collapsed, burying dozens of people in its debris. Cutters had to be deployed to extract the bodies from the ruins. Awasthi remembers personally pulling out several bodies—eighteen to nineteen people died, while only two to three survived.

It was one of the biggest industrial accidents in India. All India Radio covered it extensively the day after the accident, and then pulled the news off air completely the next day. Awasthi doesn't know why.

This incident taught him a big lesson. Henceforth, he would focus on safety first in whatever he did; all else would come later. He hasn't forgotten this lesson even after half a century. All IFFCO plants have a safety officer, ambulances, fire extinguishers, and other related materials and equipment to ensure that accidents don't happen and that there is minimal loss of life (if, nonetheless, one does occur).

Rekha: wife, partner and friend for life

Early in 1970, his brother-in-law, Murli Dhar Pandey, husband of his eldest sister Vidya, received a proposal: Shrilal Shukla, the noted Hindi litterateur and celebrated author of the path-breaking novel *Raag Darbari*, was looking for a match for his daughter, Rekha (who shares her name with Awasthi's younger sister).

That year, in January, Shrilal Shukla had been honoured with the Sahitya Akademi Award for *Raag Darbari*. The award and the popularity of the novel had given him a cult status. As a result, there was great excitement in the Awasthi and Pandey clans when Murli Dhar brought this proposal to the family.

Awasthi had decided to get married when his salary crossed ₹1,000 per month. In January 1970, his employer increased his salary to ₹1,100 per month. Awasthi, thus, gave his consent to proceed to the next level of negotiations with the family.

Shrilal Shukla, an Indian Administrative Service (IAS) officer who lived in Lucknow, wrote to him saying he wanted to discuss his daughter's marriage. Awasthi wrote back, advising him to take the Frontier Mail, adding that he would meet him in front of the station's first-class waiting room.

He had, in the meantime, bought a Lambretta scooter with a loan from his employer. He took his future father-in-law, who had come to Kota immediately after receiving the Sahitya Akademi Award, to his house in Ballabh Bari. It was a shared accommodation, but it was still very impressive—there were chandeliers, two cooks, one for non-vegetarian and the other for vegetarian fare.

Awasthi and three others, each earning ₹1,100 per month—a princely sum in those days—were staying there. So, it was quite natural for the house to wear a lavish air.

Shrilal Shukla was vegetarian. So Awasthi had food prepared accordingly. He had seen a photograph of Rekha, in which she looked quite tall, and asked him if she was taller than he. Shrilal Shukla assured him that she wasn't. Awasthi agreed to the marriage.

His future father-in-law was planning to leave that very evening and wanted to buy the local silk sarees for which Kota was famous. Awasthi took him to Kwatra Saree House next to Rajoria Store. This shop sold more than just sarees. He and his colleagues had bought trouser materials and shirt pieces as well from there and knew the owner well.

Awasthi told the owner to show sarees to Shrilal Shukla. The bill came to about ₹200, which Shukla didn't have.

Awasthi intervened and said: 'Pack the sarees. He will pay later.'

Shrilal Shukla was impressed with his presence of mind and his ability to manage potentially tricky situations. This boy is smart, he thought. But this also worried him. His daughter Rekha was a simple girl. Would they be compatible as a couple?

Soon thereafter, Awasthi and his younger sister, Rekha, went to Lucknow to meet them. The two Rekhas hit it off well, and struck up a friendly conversation. Awasthi barely got a few words in.

On his way out, he realized he had left a strip of Strepsils anti-cough lozenges behind and went back to retrieve them. His future wife was standing on their doorstep with them. The looks they exchanged in that fleeting moment convinced Awasthi that she was the girl he wanted to spend his life with.

Then, another unexpected roadblock suddenly appeared on the horizon.

Some of Shrilal Shukla's relatives objected to the match on account of Awasthi's dark complexion. 'Papa [Shrilal Shukla], too, wasn't much in favour of the marriage. But my mother-in-law put her foot down and said the marriage would take place,' Awasthi said.

It was March. Awasthi wanted a December wedding, but December was still many months away. Shrilal Shukla didn't want to wait that long; he wanted an immediate wedding.

Awasthi married Rekha, nee Shukla, on 26 June 1970. After a five-day honeymoon in Nainital, Rekha returned to her parental home to complete her MA in Hindi. She went to meet Awasthi in Kota in December during her winter vacation, when the weather in Kota is very pleasant. Rekha is an excellent singer and so, it wasn't at all surprising that she became very popular among Awasthi's friends and colleagues during the month she spent with him.

'I remember we attended some party or the other on each of the thirty-odd days she spent with me that winter. Our house was already the most famous place for parties,' he said.

The Shuklas had a car—a Chevrolet. Shrilal Shukla had bought his first car when Rekha, who was called 'Golu' at home, was born. She had never before sat on a scooter. And Awasthi had never ridden with a girl before. They were driving to a party; the road wasn't very smooth and there were several potholes. Rekha fell off the scooter.

Awasthi rode on, oblivious to the fact that his wife was no longer sitting behind him. It was only after reaching his destination that he discovered her missing. Retracing his path, he found her standing by the roadside where she had fallen. She was weeping.

'Henceforth she would hold me tight whenever she rode pillion,' Awasthi said with a grin.

Rekha went to stay with Awasthi in Kota only after completing her MA in 1971. Awasthi's mother, Durgavati, also joined them in Kota.

The days passed in a haze. They lived a lavish life together.

Awasthi stayed in Kota for four years. He had joined when the levelling work was being done and left when commercial production had stabilized.

Climbing up the ranks at Zuari

One day, he met R.K. Agarwal, Maintenance Manager, Zuari Agro Chemicals, who happened to be visiting Kota. The two of them started talking, and after learning what he did, Agarwal advised him to apply for a job.

'He told us to apply…change jobs for better opportunity. I applied and got the job…in operations,' said Awasthi.

Awasthi, Rekha, his mother Durgavati, and four or five colleagues, including V.S. Khanna and T.K. Mehta, left Kota for Zuari (in Goa) on 4 July 1971. They carried lots of luggage. Awasthi's friend Arvind Baliga's father was the Chairman of the Railway Board. He had arranged an entire coach for them.

The Awasthis were the only couple in their little group. It was a memorable train journey of three days. Monsoon had broken by then. The train first pulled into Bombay (now Mumbai); from there it reached Goa via Miraj, Londa, Castle Rock and Vasco da Gama on the fourth day, amidst torrential rain.

Agarwal sent a car to fetch them. They were allotted a house from which they could see the governor's house across the Zuari river. It was very picturesque. Next to it was Dona Paula Beach, the lover's lair in Goa, much before it became a major tourist destination.

Zuari Agro Chemicals had been established by K.K. Birla in 1967 and so, it was still a relatively small company when Awasthi joined four years later.

He was posted in the plant and was allotted mostly project work at first, and then operations.

Then, there was a plan to establish a township and a plant by levelling the mountains. But, Awasthi was not in favour of knocking down the mountains. 'Since farming is possible in the mountains, why don't we follow the same here? We can build the guest house at the top, followed by the township and then the office and a workshop. Thereafter, we can set up a power plant, a urea plant and a di-ammonium phosphate (DAP)/nitrogen, phosphorus, and potassium (NPK) plant. We may also lay our own railway line near the existing one for bagging purposes,' said Awasthi. His boss Dr Sikchi was highly impressed with his brilliant idea.

Though he had, in a very short time, emerged as the prime trouble-shooter and go-to man for the senior management team, he did not yet have a cabin to himself. He, his colleagues and the rest of their teams used to sit in an open hall, where everyone had a table and a chair. There were conference rooms for meetings.

Several decades later, when he visited Zuari at the invitation of the company's management, he was shown the logs he had written. 'They were being used as a training manual,' he said.

Hectic social life

The Awasthis took to Goa like fish to water. They were allotted a charming little bungalow overlooking the sea. 'It was an exceedingly beautiful place, and the atmosphere was just wonderful,' Awasthi said.

He and Rekha were young, newly married and fun loving. They often went to the nearby villages on Saturdays and Sundays for dance parties. 'They would erect a tent and have a dance party. Alcohol was very cheap. Beer cost a rupee. A bottle of whisky would cost five rupees. I would take my wife on a scooter and go to any nearby village. We would dance and enjoy our time and spend the night in the village itself. Usually, someone or the other from Zuari Agro would be there in the village; so, we would spend the night in his house,' he remembers.

It was the month of Sawan (July–August). One day, Rekha wanted to apply mehndi on her palms. Awasthi had no idea where to source mehndi from in Goa. Rekha smiled and pointed to the hedges around their bungalow—they were mehndi plants. Awasthi plucked the leaves, made the paste and drew prilling towers on both her palms. The design became very famous among the ladies there.

Professor Awasthi

While working in Zuari, Awasthi and his friend T.K. Mehta also began teaching at a local polytechnic. The two of them would ride Awasthi's scooter to the institute; as a result, he soon became popular as Professor Awasthi. 'I trained many Goans, both boys and girls, and recruited them in Zuari Agro,' he said.

Manu and Amol are born

All the friends who had travelled with Awasthi from Kota got married one after another—V.S. Khanna, Sunil Guliyani, Raj Bharara. T.K. Mehta married Rekha's younger sister, thus making Awasthi a co-brother-in-law.

'I don't like interfering in other people's lives. So, I didn't play any part in this romance. But when you keep a young man and young woman in close proximity, there is bound to be some attraction between them. That's what happened; theirs was a love marriage,' said Awasthi.

'Shortly afterwards I went to Japan for training in operations. Toyo Engineering, the technology partner of Zuari, had a similar plant in Japan and I was sent there to learn how it functioned; the idea was to give me first-hand experience in operations. It was both my first trip abroad and the first time Zuari was sending someone to a foreign location for training. Our first child was conceived while we were in Goa. It was an accidental conception. I got the news while I was in Japan,' said Awasthi.

Anupam was born on 1 August 1972 in Lucknow. Awasthi saw him for the first time three months later. He sent an office car to pick up Rekha and Anupam. 'I was waiting for them at home. Anupam was crying loudly. He stopped wailing the moment I took him in my arms. It was instant love...He has been a father's boy ever since,' gushes Awasthi.

Time passed quickly. Awasthi was growing in the company, getting ever-more important responsibilities. Anupam had grown into a toddler. He was called 'Manu' at home. There was one more child—Sohni, Baliga's daughter. They were the only two children in their friends' group. Manu was especially popular as he would mix with people easily. So friends often took him to their houses. When Manu grew big enough to walk and play, the Awasthis decided to have their second child—this time, a planned baby. Both Rekha and he wanted a daughter.

'I remember it was the evening of Deepavali in 1975. We were in Carmo Gracias Maternity Hospital, a famous hospital in Margao. Carmo

Gracias was the name of the doctor. I was standing outside the labour room with my mother-in-law. Dr Gracias came and said: "We could not bring Lakshmi, but we have brought Ganesh." That's why we call Amol Amolijaan also. We loved him like a daughter. He was born on 3 November 1975,' Awasthi said.

Tryst with the paper industry

Meanwhile, unknown to him, forces beyond his control were at play, pushing him towards his destiny. Awasthi's boss was Dr K.K.G. Sikchi, the very competent and technically proficient vice president of the company. He was the man behind the Zuari project.

'Zuari Agro was initially built by Dr Sikchi. He was the son-in-law of B.D. Somani, the famous industrialist. He had built a young team and I was part of that. We were the people who really built the organization,' said Awasthi.

He doesn't know the details of what transpired behind the scenes, but the managing director and the works manager of the company were abruptly changed. Then, Dr Sikchi, too was transferred to the K.K. Birla Group's paper company called Fibres and Chemicals in Malaysia.

The new management team at Zuari had different priorities. It moved fast to place its own favourites in important positions across the company. People like Awasthi and other members of Dr Sikchi's team, who had practically built the company from scratch, suddenly became *persona non grata* and were made to feel like aliens in their own backyard. Awasthi was very unhappy at these developments and began looking for another job. When Dr Sikchi, who thought very highly of him, came to know of this, he offered him a job in the Delhi office of the paper company.

Gaining international exposure

Amol was born on 3 November 1975. Dr Sikchi telephoned Awasthi on 4 November. The following day, Awasthi received a telegram from him telling him to join him in Delhi as soon as possible.

'I thought it was a good opportunity to gain international exposure. I discussed it with my wife and she also liked the idea. I took Manu with me and left for Delhi the very next day. My wife was still in hospital. She stayed on in Goa for a month with my mother-in-law,' Awasthi recalls.

Fibres and Chemicals was part of the K.K. Birla Group. So, it wasn't very difficult for Awasthi to join immediately—on deputation from Zuari, because both companies were part of the same group. A few other colleagues from Zuari, handpicked by Sikchi, also followed suit.

His wife and his new-born second son joined him after a month in New Delhi, where he was staying at his younger sister Rekha's house. The government had declared Emergency and Awasthi's brother-in-law, a writer who later became president of the Delhi University Teachers' Association, had been arrested under the draconian Maintenance of Internal Security Act, under which the Indira Gandhi administration had locked up thousands of political activists and opponents. Rekha was alone during the Emergency, and Awasthi felt that she needed his presence in her life to be at peace.

His own stars, however, were on the ascendant. 'I always say my children were lucky for me. Amol's birth brought a change in our life. I moved out of the factory atmosphere and entered the corporate world and worked closely with Dr Sikchi. I got an idea of international business, how contracting is done in the intenational arena, how financing is done by international lending agencies. It was good exposure,' he said.

Awasthi worked with Dr Sikchi for a year, by the end of which he realized that he was not achieving his goal. He realized he did not want to work in the paper industry; and he came to the conclusion that the private sector was not the right place for him.

IFFCO calling

Sometime earlier, when the new management at Zuari had begun sidelining Dr Sikchi's team, Awasthi had started discussions with IFFCO. Both, IFFCO's Managing Director Paul Pothen and Marketing Director Bhojraj Singh had spoken to him. He had met them at a conference. By this time, Awasthi's fame as a bright spark and quick learner had begun to spread within the industry, and he often attended conferences and seminars. Nothing, however, had yet come of these talks when he joined the paper project.

After moving to Delhi, Awasthi re-established contact with IFFCO. Pothen and Singh offered him the job of Project Officer at the head office in New Delhi. The job involved assisting the managing director in his work. Awasthi doesn't remember his exact salary package but recalls that it was much less than what he was then earning.

His heart told him IFFCO and the fertilizer industry would be the right fit for him. It was a big risk. Though Zuari was still a small company, the K.K. Birla Group was a well-known business house and part of the iconic Birla industrial empire. IFFCO, in contrast, was then a fledgling fertilizer company in the cooperative sector that was a public sector company controlled by the government.

'I had ambitions of working for the farmers of the country. I wanted to grow in stature at the national and international levels. I wanted to do something good and substantial. So, I thought I should try to start working towards those goals,' he said.

There was no guarantee that IFFCO would offer him opportunities to give wings to his dreams. But it was certain that Zuari—and his deputation to the paper company—would not. The balance of convenience lay in favour of making the switch.

It was a leap of faith.

'I told Dr Sikchi that I was not very happy working in the paper sector, "So, please permit me to join IFFCO." He was happy with the idea and said, "Yes, go ahead." That's how I came to IFFCO,' Awasthi recounts those fateful days in the run-up to his joining the company that would make him a legend in his lifetime.

He joined IFFCO on 15 November 1976.

THREE

RISING THROUGH THE RANKS

IFFCO was still in its infancy when Awasthi joined in the last quarter of 1976. It had two operational plants—one producing urea at Kalol, near Ahmedabad, and the other producing DAP/NPK fertilizers at Kandla—both in Gujarat. A third plant for producing urea was coming up in Phulpur in Uttar Pradesh. The headquarters was a lean office in New Delhi's new business hub, Nehru Place. Awasthi reported directly to Paul Pothen, the founder managing director of IFFCO.

IFFCO was still a small organization and had a very informal atmosphere. This meant Awasthi had to juggle several balls in the air at the same time. The 1970s were the high noon of India's tryst with licences and permits; every import required multi-agency approvals and clearances. *His most important task was handling the import requirements of the Phulpur plant.* One had to first get the budget sanctioned from the Department of Expenditure and go to the Directorate General of Technical Development for clearance. After that, one had to apply to the Reserve Bank of India for foreign exchange. There used to be a Customs Controlled Import Export list for every project—each item that was to be imported had to be listed, and prior clearance from the customs authorities was mandatory. There was a penalty if the consignment arrived without prior clearance.

Besides the Phulpur project, Awasthi was also assigned other small projects like the installation of a dry ice plant at Kalol (as the unit there had some surplus carbon dioxide). There was an old dry ice plant in The Fertilisers and Chemicals Travancore Limited, which was not being utilized. Awasthi had to get that plant installed at Kalol and produce dry ice.

'Except for these assignments, there was not much action. I assisted Mr Pothen, attended meetings with him in different government departments, prepared documents for him, briefed him on the meetings and did whatever other tasks he gave me,' Awasthi recalls.

Cabin, secretary and car

IFFCO moved its head office to a new building at 34 Nehru Place, called IFFCO House, in 1977. The change of address proved lucky for Awasthi. In recognition of his importance in the company, he was allotted a cabin on the same floor as Mr Pothen. The icing on the cake—he also got a secretary. It was the first time in his career that he had either. These were clear indicators that his career was on the fast track. He was only thirty-two.

The year 1977 was all the more memorable for Awasthi as he bought his first car that year—a second-hand Fiat.

'I drove my family to Agra and showed my mother and children the Taj Mahal and Fatehpur Sikri. We stayed the night at Agra and drove on to Kanpur,' said Awasthi, who vividly remembers the registration number of that car.

Remover of hurdles

Awasthi had made himself indispensable to Mr Pothen within a few months of joining IFFCO. Whenever something was to be purchased, Mr Pothen would refer the file to him. Though he was still relatively junior in the hierarchy, he played a key role in the purchase of office space in Lucknow's Gokhale Marg.

IFFCO started negotiating two contracts, and one of them was with Hindustan Zinc. It was thinking of putting up a phosphoric acid plant because leaching produces sulphuric acid when zinc is made. If one opts for Rajasthan rocks (raw material), then one can produce phosphoric acid. And IFFCO was interested in buying some.

Simultaneously, IFFCO opened negotiations with the Republic of Nauru to set up a phosphoric acid plant in that country. It also started considering plans for a phosphoric acid plant in Kandla, Gujarat, where it already had a phosphatic unit. 'We thought we would put up one more plant. So, we started looking for land near Kandla port,' said Awasthi.

But the management dropped the idea of setting up a plant in India as it was found to be uneconomical. Around that time, several new plants had started coming up in countries like Tunisia and Morocco. This meant there was enough—and more—supply of phosphoric acid in the global market. Perhaps because of this, Hindustan Zinc no longer seemed keen on setting up a phosphoric acid plant. And the talks with Nauru also fell through. But IFFCO expanded the Kandla plant. That was when the company started concentrating on setting up a plant in Senegal.

It was Awasthi who wrote the project report for the Senegal plant. 'I am a quick learner and I learnt how to deal with the government, how to get our jobs done, how not to waste time. If a job was given to me, I made sure it was done on time. If any officer said he would do something today, I had to make sure that he kept his word and did not stretch the delivery of his promise to the next day. That is how the utility of a person is judged,' he said.

Awasthi had cracked the code of corporate success. 'When people start working, they should always remember that the top man looks for someone who can clear hurdles,' he said. 'I quickly made friends in the government at the levels of section officers, undersecretaries, deputy secretaries and directors. At that time, joint secretaries were big officers whom only managing directors of companies could meet. Secretaries were beyond the reach of even managing directors,' he adds.

Growing respect for IFFCO

Those were the days of sloth and inefficiency. There was a law that penalized factory owners with stiff fines and even jail terms if they ran their plants at more than 100 per cent capacity utilization. Not surprisingly, most companies had substantially lower levels of efficiency.

'People began respecting IFFCO because it started running its plants at 100 per cent efficiency. It also started putting up plants in time. By this time, Mr Pothen had become a respected figure in the fertilizer industry. Its prominence was bolstered by the fact that IFFCO acquired its own corporate office. Of course, it was a very small office when you compare it with the present one, but the image makeover had started happening,' said Awasthi.

In terms of sheer performance, IFFCO was in a league of its own. It was the first Indian company to set up a purge gas recovery system at the Kalol plant. It had also set up a hydrolyser system to recover ammonia from wastewater.

All these things started happening after Awasthi joined. Before that, no one had thought of recovering something valuable from the effluent of the plant. 'We started thinking like engineers,' he said, in line with his lifelong dream of helping India become a modern nation.

Mr Pothen had a broad vision for IFFCO and the Indian fertilizer industry, and so did Awasthi. 'We had a meeting of minds,' he said. That was one of the reasons why the two of them clicked, despite the huge difference in their age and seniority.

IFFCO's Gurgaon township and the birth of IFFCO Chowk

IFFCO had very spacious, well-laid-out townships at its plants, but did not have one in Delhi-NCR, where its head office was located because of the prohibitively high cost of land in the capital. The housing loan scheme it had introduced had not picked up because the amount on offer was not sufficient for a plot or a flat in Delhi.

Mr Pothen started looking for a plot for a township in the areas adjoining Delhi. He entrusted Awasthi the responsibility of finding a suitable location. One day, Awasthi took a company car and drove to Gurgaon via the Mehrauli–Gurgaon Road.

He saw a large tract of land—where IFFCO Chowk now stands. It was next to the Gurgaon (now Gurugram) Air Force Station. The land was unencumbered. IFFCO negotiated with the Government of Haryana for 20 acres of land. The price: ₹41.7 lakh. The payment terms were easy: 25 per cent had to be paid upfront and the balance in six annual instalments. The land was acquired in September 1978.

It was decided that the township would have two distinct parts. One part, of 10 acres, was earmarked for the Fertilizer Marketing Development Institute and official residences. The remaining 10 acres was set aside for employees to buy plots and build their own houses.

Awasthi recalls how it was an enormous task to sell those plots to IFFCO employees. He first had to form a cooperative society, then get members for it, and then convince people to buy the plots. 'I took the initiative and my wife bought a 500 yard plot; then requested Mr Pothen to take one, and Finance Director Mr Ramdas to take another. With persuasion and requests, I roped in the top officers.'

Everyone was reluctant to invest because land prices had remained stagnant in Gurgaon since a long time. 'People used to say, "What have you bought!?! Where have you gone!?! Not even grass is growing there. Nobody will go there. It's a waste of money." It was typical Indian cynicism, you know,' said Awasthi with a smile. It's a completely different story now. IFFCO Chowk and the surrounding areas, including the company's township, are considered prime locations and those who own properties there consider them prized possessions.

Coming into his own

Awasthi had been promoted from F-grade to E-grade—the post is called chief manager now—within one year of joining IFFCO. He does not remember his exact designation but said he had been promoted from his position as Project Officer.

The young man who had come to Delhi looking for a job barely a decade ago was now well settled. He had a Fiat car. He had a duplex flat in Sheikh Sarai and a plot of land in Gurgaon.

But Awasthi found that money, by itself, did not motivate him; the joy of achievement was what drove him to strive harder to reach greater heights. It was an important realization—and one that came from within.

'Money is only a means. What makes you rich is your own feelings. One can feel rich even with ten rupees in one's pocket. With whatever money I had, I never felt short of money. Everything happened normally in the course of time. When there was a requirement, I purchased a scooter. When the time came, I purchased a car. Then I reached a position where the company gave me a car. Everything came on time. I get the biggest enjoyment when I am able to create something,' he said.

Today, when he looks back, he accepts, without a hint of immodesty, that the work he did in 1978 was remarkable. 'We have IFFCO Chowk and IFFCO Chowk Metro Station because of that. We have a township that we developed at a very low cost. We have the Fertilizer Marketing Development Institute where we train our marketing people. We have IFFCO Towers and IFFCO Complex, which we built when I became the managing director. So, it is the ability to create something for someone—

that is the most important thing—and that is what makes me feel really rich,' he said.

It is for these reasons he considers 1978 to be his breakout year, the year when he really came into his own and laid the foundation for everything that followed.

Earning his spurs in Hazira

The mid-1970s was a watershed period for the Indian fertilizer industry. The first oil price shock of 1973 had sent the prices of fertilizers soaring to unprecedented levels. Since fertilizers were a crucial component of the Green Revolution, critical for India's food security, the government introduced subsidies on fertilizers to make them affordable for farmers.

Around this time, a very large offshore oil-field was discovered in the Arabian Sea, off the coast of Bombay, called Bombay High. Following this discovery, the first cross-country gas pipeline, known as the Hazira–Vijaipur–Jagdishpur (HVJ) gas pipeline, was conceived to supply gas for industrial and domestic use in different parts of the country.

Six new fertilizer plants were also conceived along the route of this pipeline. Since laying the pipelines was going to take time, it was decided that some large new urea plants would be set up in close proximity to Bombay High to make use of the available gas.

Rashtriya Chemicals and Fertilizers Limited (RCF) was allotted a urea plant at Thal in the coastal town of Alibaug near Bombay. IFFCO and National Fertilizers Limited (NFL) were asked to set up a urea plant each at Hazira, a transhipment port in the Surat district of Gujarat.

IFFCO began work immediately on selecting technology for the plant. A high-powered committee was appointed, of which Mr Pothen was a member. That committee appointed two sub-committees—one for the ammonia plant and the other for the urea plant. Awasthi was a member of the sub-committee for the urea plant.

By this time, he was recognized as someone who could take the initiative and deliver. As a member of the sub-committee, he worked very diligently to understand all the nuances of the project. He wrote the whole chapter on urea technology transfer in a report for the sub-committee, which included four to five agreements. Those agreements were vetted by the Government of India, by the law ministry and by top-notch lawyers, and found to be good.

'I had acquired the acumen to negotiate and draft agreements. Even today, those agreements are the backbone (of Krishak Bharati Cooperative Limited [KRIBHCO]). So that was the level of my involvement,' he said, adding that his sub-committee had to select the technology and facilitate its transfer from the foreign consultant to Projects and Development India Limited (PDIL), its Indian counterpart. The idea was to make PDIL self-sufficient in designing and implementing fertilizer projects later.

The sub-committee selected Snamprogetti's technology. Awasthi took the call for the plant to have two streams—mirror images of each other. 'The advantage was that these could be operated with only one control room. The consultant did not have to redesign the second stream,' said Awasthi.

Awasthi got deeply involved in the project and was appointed head of the urea plant to manage this project. He went to Snamprogetti's head office in Milan, stayed there for three months with his team and finalized the design of the urea plant.

Though he was still in the middle management cadre, he was by this time involved in the management of the company, along with Mr Pothen and Mr Krishnan, executive director of IFFCO, who was in-charge of the Hazira Fertilizer Project. In this capacity, he played a role in land acquisition as well.

They went to Surat to acquire the land. 'There was a tree, and Mr Pothen said, "Oh, this is the sehar tree." The tree that had come from Africa. We protected that tree. We took care to protect the environment many decades before it became fashionable to do so,' he said.

Baroda (now Vadodara) became the centre for the technology transfer from Snamprogetti to PDIL because of its proximity to Surat.

'It gives me great pleasure that the plant, now under KRIBHCO, is running very well. It's a very well-operated plant,' said Awasthi.

From IFFCO to KRIBHCO and back

Mr Pothen left IFFCO in 1980 and became the managing director of KRIBHCO. That year, the plant became a part of KRIBHCO, and IFFCO's Hazira Project Implementation Committee was dissolved. Awasthi and other members of the recently dissolved sub-committees were drafted into the new company.

Recounting the events that led to the formation of KRIBHCO, Awasthi said: 'Mr Pothen had this dilemma from the very beginning—should we have the plant in IFFCO, or should we form another cooperative? We started working on having a cooperative agro group and we thought that we can have this plant in Surat and call it a different multi-state cooperative [...] The idea was to create a chain of fertilizer cooperatives.'

That was what Mr Pothen's great friend Verghese Kurien had done with Amul, one of India's most famous home-grown brands. But Amul does not produce milk; it gets its supplies from as many cooperatives and is primarily a marketing company. Similarly, Mr Pothen wanted to position IFFCO as a brand of fertilizers—produced by IFFCO, KRIBHCO and several other cooperatives to be set up in the future—that would have a common marketing team.

Despite his high regard for Mr Pothen, Awasthi had reservations about this plan. He was convinced that setting up KRIBHCO was a bad idea. 'I think Mr Pothen got a little scared about IFFCO becoming too big. He was perhaps worried about being able to manage plants with such diverse technology sources...But that was probably not the right decision.'

Perhaps Mr Pothen wanted to avoid following in the footsteps of the Fertilizer Corporation of India Ltd., which had grown big and unwieldy and had almost collapsed under the weight of its own size. It was the era when small was considered beautiful and Awasthi feels his mentor may have been persuaded by the rhetoric that accompanied the slogan.

Awasthi apprehended conflict between the two cooperatives, and he was proved right. When KRIBHCO was formed, the idea was that IFFCO and KRIBHCO would have common marketing. That did happen for some time. But then, in the name of creating job opportunities for more people, the marketing functions were separated, and that's when the competition between the two cooperatives started.

The vision with which KRIBHCO had been created was not followed. 'The only solution, which I always thought was the right one, was that the Hazira plant should have remained with IFFCO. Had IFFCO and KRIBHCO remained together, then all that conflict in the cooperative sector would not have been there. Cooperatives would probably have played a major role in the industrialization of the country, which was hampered because of the competition that was created,' he said, speaking with passion so many decades after KRIBHCO was carved out of IFFCO.

Mr Pothen retired from KRIBHCO in late 1981 or 1982. The government approved plans for IFFCO to set up a new urea plant at Aonla in Uttar Pradesh around that time. In February 1983, Srinivas Reddy, the then chairman of IFFCO, approached Awasthi to return and take charge of building the new plant.

'I wrote the project report of KRIBHCO; I even selected its name to rhyme with IFFCO. I was part of the core team with Mr Pothen and Mr Krishnan that ran it. But I felt KRIBHCO was too small an organization for me. I looked at it as an offshoot of IFFCO. In my heart of hearts, I always wanted to come back to IFFCO. So, when the opportunity came, I returned,' he said simply.

At that time, IFFCO was facing severe headwinds. It was facing instability at the top. Several part-time managing directors had come and gone. The chairman was not a technical person; he was a big politician, close to the former prime minister.

For the second time in seven years, Awasthi took a leap of faith and joined IFFCO in 1983—this time as project manager, in charge of the Aonla project. Shortly after that, Mr M.H. Avdhani came on board as managing director from the Southern Petrochemical Industries Corporation (SPIC) where he had been vice president.

In 1986, Awasthi became the joint general manager, a post that was created for him. Since he was also the project manager, he carried the same authority as a general manager.

This was when his career really took off.

Working on three projects simultaneously

Avdhani was still relatively young and very energetic. He had a vision and a desire to do something big. He took an immediate liking to Awasthi and practically handed over the entire planning and execution of the Aonla project to him.

The new managing director was from southern India and wasn't fluent in Hindi. He could make himself understood in the language, but displayed a visible lack of felicity in its usage. He needed somebody who could speak Hindi fluently.

Awasthi stepped into this breach. He already had experience of liaising with the government. He was young and hard-working, and he had very good relationships with several people in the government. 'So, we got on very well. And that is where the real manager in me began to take off,' he said with a flourish.

In 1983–1984, IFFCO started work on three projects simultaneously. One was the Aonla project. The second was Godavari Fertilizers. And the third was Industries Chimiques du Senegal (ICS). This last project had been conceived earlier, but the approval to participate in its equity, along with SPIC and the Government of India, came in 1983. IFFCO agreed to buy the phosphoric acid that the Senegal plant produced.

For Godavari Fertilizers, Srinivas Reddy, Mr Avdhani and Awasthi went to meet N.T. Rama Rao, who had just won the state election and become Chief Minister of Andhra Pradesh. He greeted them very cordially and agreed to the proposal for IFFCO to hold 25 per cent in the company and for the Andhra Pradesh government to have 26 per cent. The complex, which would produce DAP/NPK, would be based on imported phosphoric acid.

'I am very happy that you are coming to Andhra Pradesh,' Rama Rao said and broke into Telugu with Srinivas Reddy and Avdhani, both of whom were native Telugu speakers. Awasthi couldn't follow a word of what was spoken

'I was now extensively involved in three projects—Aonla, Godavari Fertilizers and ICS Senegal. The first shipment of acid from Senegal reached Kandla sometime in May 1984. That month, the Industrial Development Bank of India approval for financing Godavari Fertilizers was received.

Getting started on Aonla

IFFCO started discussions with the Overseas Economic Cooperation Fund, the Japanese financial institution, the Asian Development Bank and the Danish International Development Agency. Those were pre-liberalization days, when foreign exchange transactions were negotiated along with the government—not directly. Awasthi was part of all those discussions.

The company also started negotiating with the Oil and Natural Gas Corporation for the supply of gas. The total project cost was ₹730 crore; the foreign component was ₹277 crore, and the Indian component was

₹453 crore. The Government of India approval for it was received during the last quarter of 1984.

Awasthi vividly remembers going to meet N.D. Tiwari, the then Chief Minister of Uttar Pradesh, for the acquisition of land for the Aonla complex. He had been chairman of the committee that had selected the sites for the six fertilizer plants that were being planned along the route of the HVJ pipeline. He summoned the Chief Secretary and asked him to immediately handover the land to IFFCO. This was done in a very short time.

When Awasthi went to Aonla to see the site, he saw a faqir sitting near a mazar. He asked him: 'I am taking this land, what will happen?'

The man said, 'Rest assured. Just leave this space undisturbed.'

Awasthi promised him he would. 'We kept the mazar intact and developed a nursery there.'

But within days of starting work on the site, Awasthi faced his first major challenge: the allotted land had sand one metre in and it was also in an earthquake-prone zone. This required extensive piling work to be done, but what kind? There was no Google in those days, so extensive research was needed on how to stabilize the land for the proposed factory and the adjoining township.

Awasthi worked closely with Avdhani to solve this problem. 'We tried to find out which company had the technology. We also toyed with the idea of shifting the site. But by that time, substantial work had already taken place on the site. So, the first major work we did was to solve this problem,' said Awasthi, relishing his achievement even after all these years.

The Aonla project had been on a fast track from the very beginning. A separate sub-committee had been constituted and given adequate powers to take decisions. These were later put up to the board of directors for information and ratification.

'That's how we completed the Aonla project within schedule,' said Awasthi, who was a member of the sub-committee initially only as a special invitee (as he was not a member of the board). As a special invitee, he presented the proposals before the sub-committee, which held its first meeting in April 1985. The Godavari Fertilizers project was also in full swing. The Senegal plant had already been commissioned by then.

Snamprogetti and Haldor Topsøe (now Topsoe, a Danish company) were the technology suppliers for the urea and ammonia plants, respectively. PDIL was the joint consultant for the detailed engineering.

Awasthi used the template for the Hazira plant for his project. The technology agreements were based on the earlier terms. It was also agreed that as the owner's representative, the foreign consultant and the joint consultant would be there to supervise and be party to any decision taken. IFFCO would, of course, have the final say on all issues.

'The concept was that it should be shoulder to shoulder and back to back so that there were no grey areas,' recalls Awasthi.

There was also the condition that the plant should operate at certain minimum loads and the energy consumption should not exceed a certain level. All those things were defined and there were penalties for failing to meet the agreed benchmarks. However, these have never had to be exercised as the plant has always functioned within the set parameters.

The Aonla project was in full swing. The zero date had already elapsed. 'Those were hectic days,' Awasthi said. 'We were working twenty-four seven. Those days, documentation was very important. Our job was to prepare all the documents that were needed.'

He first had to get the managing director to sign-off on the documents. Then, the documents had to be explained to all the government directors on the board, the Department of Fertilizers, the Ministry of Agriculture, the Planning Commission and the Ministry of Finance.

That is how he caught the eye of the Secretary, Department of Fertilizers, who handpicked him to head PPCL in 1986. He was only forty-one years old then.

So, 1986 was another landmark year in his career. He was promoted from project manager, Aonla project, to joint general manager in IFFCO in February 1986. Then, in October that year, he was appointed chairman-cum-managing director (CMD) of PPCL.

Aonla was commissioned in May 1988. Avdhani sent Awasthi a special invitation to attend the function, and the plant was dedicated to the nation by the then Prime Minister of India, Rajiv Gandhi.

'If you see the facility, you will realize the expanse of the plant. There is a well-laid-out township and the plant has adequate facilities and support systems. We designed the plant with Avdhani in such a manner that it can have two streams of ammonia plant and four streams of urea plant,' he said with obvious pride.

Amma's death

Awasthi was well settled in Delhi by the mid-1980s. The larger Awasthi family had moved on after absorbing the shock of Devi Shanker's premature death. Kamlesh Awasthi's children had also found their niches and were doing very well for themselves. Rekha, the youngest among the Awasthi siblings, was teaching Hindi literature in Delhi University. Amma now lived mostly with Awasthi in his duplex flat in Sheikh Sarai, in south Delhi.

It was 4 May 1985. The Awasthis had retired to bed after dinner. Their domestic help knocked on his door and told Awasthi that his mother was calling him downstairs. She lived on the floor below.

He rushed down with his wife, Rekha. Durgavati was lying on her bed. She said, in Hindi, 'My time has come to leave this world. Help me lie down on the floor.' Awasthi and his wife did so.

Then she said: 'No, wait. The lunar eclipse is about to be over. I should take a bath.' Turning to her daughter-in-law, she added, 'You tend to forget (these rituals). There is gold and tulsi leaves kept in a wrap. Gangajal is also there. Put them in my mouth.'

Awasthi and his wife did as they were told as she lay on the floor. Then, she asked to see Awasthi's two sons—her grandsons.

Awasthi was distraught. He wanted to rush her to hospital immediately, but she would have none of it. 'There is no point…my time has come.'

Her doctor was called, and she was then rushed to the hospital. She had begun to lose consciousness by this time. At around 5.00 a.m. the next day, at eighty years of age, Durgavati passed away, holding her son's hand.

Awasthi said that he has inherited his mother's strength of character, generosity and never-say-die spirit. 'She never discouraged me from doing anything. We did not have much money. She sold her jewellery to pay for our education. She also got her eldest daughter married by selling her jewellery. But she never objected when I gave away my clothes and other things to anyone. She allowed me to grow organically. She was an exemplary lady. She faced life with dignity and died a happy mother,' he said.

Proving his mettle at PPCL

PPCL is a public sector mining company that was teetering on the brink of closure. The company had pyrite mines in Bihar and Rajasthan and rock phosphate mines in the Doon Valley, then in Uttar Pradesh, and now in Uttarakhand. The company, with 2,000 employees, had been incurring losses for a long time and people were deeply concerned that this might force the company to shut down.

In 1986, a revival package was drawn up, which proposed setting up a pyrite-based single super phosphate (SSP) plant in Bihar and mechanizing the process at all of PPCL's mines. Awasthi was chosen to be the CMD of PPCL to execute this revival plan.

K.D. Vasudeva was the Secretary in the Department of Fertilizers. 'He told me, "Awasthi, you are doing very good work in Aonla. PPCL is a mining company that has been sick for a long time. I want you to revive it."'

Awasthi appeared for the interview conducted to select the CMD of PPCL. He was selected. A ₹45 crore revival package had been approved by Parliament a few days before that.

Awasthi was a little apprehensive. He was still young and had no experience in the mining sector. He told Vasudeva: 'Sir, I am only forty-one years old; my children are small. If the company closes, what will be my future?'

But Vasudeva would have none of it. He said: 'You can revive the company; you go and join.'

'Sir, my managing director is not in town, who shall I give my resignation to?'

'You resign over the phone,' Vasudeva ordered.

'Those days fertilizer secretaries used to be very powerful officers. I spoke to Mr Avdhani from his phone and joined PPCL the very next day. Mr Vasudeva did not want the company to close, so he gave me all his support in reviving PPCL. He helped me get an appointment with Rajiv Gandhi-ji, supported me in getting the budget for the project enhanced and also helped me establish myself at PPCL. He had confidence in me,' said Awasthi.

Awasthi set a feverish pace at work from day one. He summoned R.P. Singh, who was Manager, Personnel and Administration, PPCL, from Dehri-on-Sone.

'He wanted all the data relating to employees—how many people were there in each grade, the structure of the company, the recruitment policy, the promotion policy, etc. At the end of this intense grilling session, he said, "Your recruitment policy is not clear. A new policy will have to be made,"' recalls Singh, who later became director of HR and Legal at IFFCO.

'How many chemical engineers do we have?'

'Sir, we do not have a single chemical engineer here,' Singh replied.

Awasthi was very surprised. He said, 'It's such a big organization; there are nearly 2,000 people working here, but we do not have even one chemical engineer?'

'Sir, this is a mining company, so there are mostly mining people. There are some mechanical and electrical engineers for the maintenance and upkeep of mining machines and equipment; the rest are all labourers.'

'This is a major challenge. We have to set up a new plant and run it. We need people who have the ability to do this work.'

Awasthi ordered a project report to be prepared for the SSP plant. When he saw the report, he said, 'The person who has made this report doesn't have any experience of running a plant.'

He made all the calculations sitting there and told Singh: 'We will have to take at least two hundred trained people from outside to set up and run the plant. You will have to recruit these two hundred people within the next three months.'

It was Singh's turn to be taken aback. 'Sir, this is too short a period to do that,' he said,

'Why?'

'In the public sector, there is a set procedure that is followed for recruitments. First, an advertisement is placed in a newspaper, and thirty days are given to apply. Then, shortlisting takes place and letters for interviews are issued. A minimum of fifteen days is given to appear for the interview. Then, after the selection, three months' time is given for joining. It is just not possible to recruit so many people in three months.'

Awasthi was not a man to let archaic procedures come in the way of his plans. 'If you can't work at my speed then I will have to look for someone else to get me what I want,' he said, sending a chill down Singh's spine.

This was to be Awasthi's first clash with 'established procedures'. And it marked the first of dozens of instances over his career when he used a common-sense approach to cut through red tape in order to achieve his goals.

Said Singh, 'Awasthi gave us all the freedom to devise ways and means to find the best professionals. He said, "These two hundred professionals will be the crucial people who will bear the plant like pillars." He gave us a wonderful clue. He said, "You first hire the general manager and the deputy general manager and then ask them to find the best professionals they know."'

The idea worked. That's how the whole chain of professionals, from general manager to linesmen, was recruited. Each layer selected the one below it. They were told, 'You are the masters of your field. Now you select the best people to assist you.'

When candidates came for interviews, the selected ones were given appointment letters the same day. The speed with which the recruitment was completed left everyone surprised.

Then, Awasthi changed the culture of the company by overhauling the interior design of the corporate office—from dark brown walnut interiors with lots of cabins to cedar-panelled low-height partitioned workstations with only three cabins—for himself, for the finance director and for the executive director. This made the office environment very lively.

Awasthi also changed the way the office functioned. T.N. Jaggi, who had been CMD before Awasthi, had been retained as an adviser to the CMD. He would attend office every day. Awasthi had asked Jaggi to conduct a meeting with a consultant. Before the meeting started, Jaggi asked the new CMD to come for the meeting.

Awasthi said, 'My presence is not required in the meeting.'

'Then how will you know what happened in the meeting.'

'You are conducting the meeting, the technical director is there with you, the finance director is also there. Why is my presence necessary? I have full faith in my team. You brief me about the meeting later,' Awasthi said.

It had never happened before that the CMD did not attend a technical meeting. This incident had a huge impact on the morale of the team. They started believing that the new CMD had faith in them.

After taking stock of the company, Awasthi estimated that PPCL would need an additional 40 acres of land for the project.

'Acquiring 40 acres of land will be a huge challenge,' Singh told him.

'The plant cannot be set up without that,' Awasthi replied, adding that he would visit Amjhore for an on-the-spot survey.

Meeting a mafia don

Awasthi travelled by train to Dehri-on-Sone, the railhead nearest to Amjhore. Surya Dev Singh was a very powerful don of the coal mafia in the Dhanbad belt. He occupied the berth opposite Awasthi's, and his bodyguards, armed with pistols and guns, occupied the remaining two berths of the first-class compartment. The PPCL chief thought to himself: where have I come?

After a while, the two of them struck up a conversation. 'Sir, you are travelling with such protection; who are you?' Awasthi asked.

'I am Surya Dev Singh. My enemies are always on the lookout to kill me. That's why my booking is never done in my name. You can see, this booking is not in my name.'

'But people can find you even if you do not make bookings in your name. They can still find ways to harm you.'

'No, no! My bodyguards will never let anyone come near me.'

'Do you think a person hell-bent on killing you will be intimidated by your bodyguards? He can prick you with a poisoned pin and take your life.'

'Yes, you are right.'

'It's God who gives and takes lives.'

Then the mafia don asked: 'Where are you going?'

Awasthi told him about his new appointment and the purpose of his visit.

Singh said, 'Oh, that's a Naxalite-infested area. You will have to be very careful. You will also require bodyguards for your protection.' He offered his new-found companion food.

Awasthi ate with him, believing the food to be safe.

It was a memorable journey with Surya Dev Singh.

Getting down to business at PPCL

The office in Dehri-On-Sone had some residential rooms. It was standard operating procedure to proceed there from the station, freshen up, ascertain whether there was peace in Amjhore and then set out for the site. Awasthi asked Singh if there was a guest house in Amjhore. On being told there was, he said, 'Let's go there straight away.'

An hour's drive got them there. Awasthi saw the plant, met the office people and stayed the night there. The next morning, he went into the township to meet the people. Everyone looked at him as if he were Nadir Shah because news had spread that retrenchment would take place. Everyone seemed anxious and upset.

Awasthi called all the employees for a meeting that afternoon. 'Look, if you are ready to cooperate with me, then I will also try and ensure that no one loses his job,' Awasthi told them.

Everyone agreed to cooperate.

'Will you do whatever I ask you to do? If I ask you to dig a lake here, will you do that?'

They said, 'Yes.'

'One more thing: whoever is above fifty-five years should honestly reveal his age…You all will plant a tree here every day and we will dig a lake here.'

Everyone agreed to come on board.

Then he sent a message to the Naxalite leaders that he wanted to talk to them. Everyone knew each other there, so getting the message across did not prove difficult.

'Before we begin work, I wish to seek the cooperation of those who believe in guns. If they say yes, then we will work; if they say no, then we will not work,' Awasthi told them.

A frank discussion followed with the Naxalite leaders. The new CMD assured them that the project would benefit the local people. 'We will first ask the Government of India to withdraw the retrenchment proposal. Then we will ask for an additional budget so that we can set up a good plant here.'

Awasthi's predecessor had proposed a budget of ₹158 crore. He said: 'I will set up the plant at ₹100 crore, but to do that I require everyone's cooperation. You people will have to do this. I will only bring the technology. We will have to work very honestly because there is not enough money. If you are ready, if you are also ready to give us the additional land that we require, then I am ready to do this work.'

Everyone again agreed.

Meeting with Rajiv Gandhi

Girish Narayan Mishra was a famous trade union leader of those times. He was also the election agent of Jagjivan Ram. Bindeshwari Dube was the Chief Minister of Bihar at that time. Awasthi took both of them with him and went to meet Rajiv Gandhi.

He told the prime minister, 'It's a Naxalite-infested area and there is extreme poverty there. If the company closes down, three to four thousand people will become jobless. We will have a major problem there. You give me ₹98 crore; I will set up the plant.'

Then he briefly explained the plan he had in mind. The chief minister said he would provide all the required support to the company. Mishra said he would ensure the backing of all the workers.

Rajiv Gandhi said, 'Wait a minute,' and went inside.

'I will give you ₹78 crore; ₹20 crore will be in a contingency fund. You will have to take the approval of the Ministry of Finance to spend that. I am also withdrawing the retrenchment proposal,' he said upon his return.

Work began at the site shortly after that. PPCL had to take some professionals from outside because the company had only employed mining experts; there was no one who could set up and manage the plant.

Awasthi would visit Amjhore thrice, sometimes even four times, every month. His flight would reach Patna airport at 8.15 p.m. and at 8.30 p.m. he would start out for Amjhore. The whole area was full of Naxalites. His would be the only vehicle on the road, but he was never harmed. He would reach Amjhore shortly after midnight, spend a day or two there, finish his work, return to Patna, give a report to the chief minister and fly back to New Delhi.

Mastery over project management

Awasthi brought the lessons he had learned at Zuari and IFFCO, first under Dr Sikchi then under Mr Pothen and finally as the person in charge of the Aonla project, to the Amjhore project. Three other traits he displayed in ample measure were: a disarming candour, an almost prescient foresight, and a raw courage in the face of great personal danger.

Among the first things Awasthi did was to go get a buy-in from the unions. Going against the advice of his senior team, he assured the unions that no one would lose their jobs.

The union leaders said, 'If we do not lose our jobs, then we are ready to do whatever you say. We will never let you down.'

Then Awasthi set about acquiring 40 acres of land. He was a man in a hurry, and he did not have time for the snail-paced procedures of the public sector. So, he decided to acquire the land under emergency provisions.

The villagers were called and told, 'Whoever gives his land will get employment in the company. Lots of trucks will start plying for the movement of goods. You will get business opportunities.'

Many rounds of meetings were held. The prominent people of the village were taken into confidence. Eventually, they saw the benefits that would accrue and agreed to give their land. The District Magistrate of Rohtas played a stellar role in the negotiations. It was he who suggested that since the paperwork would take time, we should meanwhile proceed with the acquisition of land for the Amjhore project by giving 80 per cent advance to the farmers.

Awasthi did this and started work immediately. But his unconventional, albeit legal, methods gave rise to a peculiar problem—no one in the government could believe that so much work, and especially land acquisition, could be done in one month. They suspected a scam.

A two-member committee was formed to investigate the matter. This committee looked at the project in granular detail—tender documents, purchase orders, bills—they looked at everything and were very impressed. They wrote a very favourable report.

Awasthi's problem-solving and project implementation skills were again on display when it came to the disposal of low-grade pyrite, called shale, a by-product of mining high-grade pyrite, which contains sulphur and degrades the soil. The sulphur that seeped out of the pyrite was going into the wells. The structure is as follows: there are steep hills on one side, the plant is in the middle and down below is the Sone River. The slope is nearly vertical. The pyrite mines are in the hills. When pyrite is mined, sulphur seeps out of it, but there was no system for its treatment. When it rained, all the water from the hills went down into the wells. The sulphur turned the soil acidic, and this had a disastrous impact on farming. As a result, there was extreme poverty in the area and Naxalism was at its peak there.

Awasthi had a plan worked out in his mind—to bring water from the Sone River and fill up the lake. The water from the lake would seep down and clean the wells by removing sulphur from the water. The idea was to make sulphuric acid from pyrite and then make SSP—which Awasthi subsequently branded as SoneGanga by borrowing the names of the two prominent rivers of the region—from sulphuric acid.

A German company called Lurgi was the technology supplier. He told them, 'We will have to find some way to use the shale or else the plant will not last long.'

They said, 'It is not possible.' In the process of making sulphuric acid, pyrite is smelted in a roaster. They said, 'The roaster cannot reach the temperature to smelt the low-grade pyrite.'

Awasthi's solution: put up an additional roaster alongside the main roaster and try to increase the temperature in the main roaster.

They liked this idea, researched it and informed Awasthi within a month that this could be done.

The additional roaster and the acquisition of 40 acres of land increased the project cost by ₹20 crore. Awasthi put his heart and soul into it and got the budget approved.

As the pyrite mining continued, the land was becoming increasingly barren. Awasthi apprehended that the local situation could turn very dangerous before the situation improved.

One day, the villagers surrounded Awasthi's car, brandishing sticks and stones. R.P. Singh was in the back seat with him.

Before the younger man could react, Awasthi, completely oblivious to the threat to his life, climbed on to the roof of the car and said loudly, 'You please listen to me. I was a big officer in a very big organization. I have been sent here with a challenge. If this project comes here, your whole area will benefit greatly from it. We will not bring people from outside to work here. You will get the jobs; you will get the opportunities to do business.'

A leader from the crowd came forward and said, 'Our fields have been ruined. We will not let anyone do anything here.'

Awasthi said, 'This project will benefit you too. But if you want to have discussions with us then you come to our office, we will sit and talk properly. We can't have discussions here like this. If you do not agree with me, then tell me here and now, I will go back today. The plant will not be set up here.'

This statement, and his display of raw courage in the face of overwhelming danger to his person, changed the mood of the crowd and they cleared the road.

When they went to the office to talk, Awasthi started firing the leader as soon as he entered. He said, 'You are a leader, and you are hell-bent on destroying the area.'

This left the poor fellow stunned. 'How can you say that? I have done so much for the area,' he said.

'Who will benefit from such protests? You do not understand and start creating a ruckus.'

This carried on for a while. In the end, the leader said, 'We will support you.' Then he started requesting jobs for his people.

Awasthi said, 'All that will come later. The jobs will come to your people only. Let us begin our work.'

This is how the issue was resolved. Work started.

All the contractors were given a mobilization advance. This was another first for PPCL. The finance director opposed the idea in the beginning.

Awasthi said, 'You take performance bonds from them, but you must give them the advance. This will add to their enthusiasm.' He issued directions that the contractors should be treated with respect and should be given all the facilities and assistance they required. All kinds of facilities were made available to the contractors on the 35 kilometre stretch between Dehri and Amjhore. Many houses were rented for them to stay.

'The enthusiasm that developed there was unparalleled,' said Singh. 'The plant was set up a month before the deadline. For the first time in the history of PPCL, the board of directors decided to give one month's extra salary to the employees as a reward for their hard work.' This practice of giving one month's extra salary continued as long as Awasthi was CMD of PPCL.

Meeting with Devi Lal

The SSP plant in PPCL was commissioned in March 1989 and in November that year, elections to the Ninth Lok Sabha were held. V.P. Singh became the Prime Minister of India and Devi Lal the deputy prime minister. Devi Lal kept the Ministry of Agriculture with him and also brought the Department of Fertilizers—earlier under the Ministry of Chemicals and Fertilizers—under his ministry. This had an impact on PPCL as well.

Amjhore falls in Sasaram constituency. Chhedi Paswan won the election there by defeating Meira Kumar, daughter of Jagjivan Ram. Paswan wanted to become president of the employees' union at PPCL and thought Awasthi was putting roadblocks in his path. This made him very angry.

Paswan accused Awasthi, a Brahmin, of practising casteism. He sent a letter, signed by several members of parliament (MPs), to the prime minister, accusing Awasthi of corruption and demanding an immediate investigation.

For the first time in his life, Awasthi experienced caste politics.

Devi Lal summoned him at once and said: '*Chhore, tu Congress ka aadmi hai* [Boy, you are a Congress man]?'

Awasthi replied in Hindi: '*Tauji, ham sarkar ke naukar hain. Tab Congress ki sarkar thi, ab aapki sarkar hai* [Sir, we are government servants. Earlier there was a Congress government, now it is your government].'

He said: '*Nahi, mujhe pakka pata hai tu Congress ka aadmi hai* [No, I know you are a Congress man].'

'*Tauji, aap bhi to Congress mein the* [Sir, you were also with the Congress once].'

Devi Lal laughed and said: '*Achha jawab dena jaanta hai* [You are quite quick-witted].'

'*Tauji, aap ek committee banao aur usse jaanch karao, agar main galat hun to mujhe nikaal dena, nahin to mujhe kaam karne dena* [Sir, you set up a committee and investigate my work. If I'm found guilty, then sack me, or else allow me to work],' Awasthi told him.

A committee was formed under the chairmanship of Upendra Nath Verma, a minister of state in the central government. Three to four MPs, including Chhedi Paswan, were members of the committee. Everyone went to Amjhore.

They held public meetings, spoke very badly about Awasthi, and said he was a Brahmin and was indulging in casteism and corruption.

But when they saw the work and all the figures, they found that everything was in order and that the company was doing very well. When they broke for lunch, Awasthi did not join them. Verma called him to join.

But Awasthi was adamant. 'They have called me casteist and corrupt, I will not join them.' Then Verma himself went and mollified him. 'Please come and have lunch with us. What we said in the meeting was because of our political compulsions. Such things happen in politics. We have seen everything. You are doing very good work. Please come.'

The committee wrote a very favourable report after they returned.

Chhedi Paswan is now with the Bharatiya Janata Party. 'We have very good relations. Such things happen in politics,' Awasthi said with a shrug.

Devi Lal, meanwhile, had obviously taken a liking to Awasthi. He would often call him to discuss the state of the fertilizer industry. And whenever they met, he would say: '*Arre, is chhore ko lassi pila* [Bring lassi for this boy].'

Mechanizing operations

PPCL also had pyrite mines in Rajasthan and rock phosphate mines in the Doon Valley. When his name was being discussed for PPCL, he had seen an advertisement in the newspaper for its Durmala mines in the Doon Valley—'Mules are needed to transport goods.' His heart sank. 'I was in an aeroplane. I thought, "Oh my God, I am a man of technology, and I am going to a place where mules carry goods."' Awasthi breaks into laughter when he recalls the incident.

As soon as he joined PPCL, he called Mr Agha, who was an expert on ropeways. 'Sir, can you make a ropeway for me?'

'Why do you want a ropeway?' Mr Agha asked.

'I can't stand mules. It's an eighteenth-century idea. I can't be the chairman of a company where mules carry goods.'

The ropeway was installed, and all the mules were discharged. This led to increased productions and higher profits at the Durmala mines. He also upgraded the company's Harawala mines.

The office in Dehradun was in a rented building. The condition of the building was very bad, and its owner wanted PPCL to vacate it. Awasthi asked him: 'Why don't you sell your property to us. We will give you as much money as you want.' The property was spread over two acres and PPCL purchased it for ₹7 lakh to ₹8 lakh.

Awasthi brushes aside criticism regarding the red tape plaguing the government. 'I did all these things on my own initiative in an institution that was completely under the control of the government. I have received full cooperation in whatever I wanted to do. Of course, I had to explain everything before the board of directors, but they supported me when they saw that positive results are coming,' he said.

His experience at IFFCO, when it was controlled by the government, was also the same. 'There were tough times also, big challenges also came, but my overall experience is that I got more cooperation than opposition.'

When he joined PPCL, he found that all the women employees wore dirty clothes. He issued uniforms for everyone. 'I ensured complete discipline. Everyone had to wear a helmet and shoes, and everyone had to follow safety instructions. I said, "I will not tolerate anything that endangers the safety and security of the people."' The images of the prilling tower collapse at Kota all those years ago remain etched in his memory and still give him the shivers.

He also wrote Powers of Officers, a document defining the powers of each grade of officers, for the first time in PPCL, which enumerated how officers would exercise their powers. He also decreed that he should receive only the bare minimum number of files. 'My job is to expand the company by planning for the future. My job is not to spend time on files for small expenses,' he said, setting a limit below which his approval would not be required.

Learning important life lessons

His experiences at PPCL taught him several important lessons that have shaped his philosophical outlook to life.

'The story of PPCL is the same as the story everywhere else. You go somewhere to bring development; there you encounter both positive and negative forces. Positive forces are dormant while negative forces dominate. You have to work, keeping in view the larger interests of the people around you. I decided to do that. If what you're doing is right, then people will support you,' he said.

'I will do what is right. I am not one to be intimidated by adversity or opponents. This trait has probably come to me from my mother. She was an absolutely fearless woman. I am not afraid of anyone and never bow my head in front of anyone except God. I speak with everyone and behave with utmost respect. But if someone thinks that he can bring me under pressure then he's sadly mistaken,' he adds.

'The power to exercise authority comes from the power within you…from your knowledge. I am inclined to learn new things. I have no hesitation in this. I am ready to learn from anyone. I learn from my grandchildren.'

Awasthi turned PPCL around. He set up a new plant that ran very well and brought huge profits to the company. He also turned around and mechanized its mining operations.

'In 1986, when I had joined, the salary component was around ₹10 crore to ₹11 crore. When I left the company in 1993, its turnover had increased to ₹300 crore to ₹400 crore, and the salary component in it had grown to just ₹30 crore to ₹40 crore,' said Awasthi.

Additional charge of RCF

In view of his good performance at PPCL, the government gave Awasthi the additional charge of RCF as CMD in 1991. RCF is an important public sector company which manufactures urea, complex fertilizers and a range of industrial chemicals. It has two manufacturing facilities, at Trombay and Thal, near Mumbai.

Public sector companies in India are categorized as Schedule A, B, C and D based on investment, capital employed, net sales, profit before tax, number of employees, number of units, national importance, level of technology, strategic importance and a number of other factors. Schedule A companies are the biggest and most important, Schedule B comes next in the pecking order, followed by Schedule C and Schedule D.

PPCL was a Schedule C company, but Awasthi was promoted to Schedule B. RCF is a Schedule A company. So, it was a huge recognition for Awasthi to be given charge of a Schedule A company. This, naturally, bred resentment among a lot of people.

'When I joined RCF, I had to face a lot of opposition. First, I was not in "peer-ranking" as I was still relatively young and not so senior.

Secondly, RCF was an organization where I could not work systematically. I like working in a systematic manner. I first organize the structure of the organization, set the parameters and define the rights and responsibilities of everyone,' said Awasthi.

At RCF, he first streamlined the organization and set everyone's responsibilities. For example, the plant at Thal did not have enough people. The junior officers were running the plant while senior officers sat in Chembur, Bombay. Awasthi changed that. Here, also, he wrote the Powers of Officers and ensured that discipline was strictly followed everywhere in the organization.

The second major problem in RCF was its militant workers' unions. There were several workers unions; one of them was the Mathadi Workers Union. Bal Thackeray was its president, and it was very aggressive. However, Awasthi never had occasion to confront Thackeray's union during his stint with the company.

The third big problem at RCF was that it seemed like the whole company was on a buying spree. Whenever he asked about it, he was told, 'It is important.'

Unlike many chief executives who prefer to spend all their time in meetings and in air-conditioned chambers, Awasthi likes to walk around his plants to get the feel of each place. He enjoys meeting young engineers and people at his plants. At RCF, he saw there were several storerooms that were locked, some of them had remained closed for years. No one seemed to know what lay behind the locked doors. Awasthi ordered the doors opened, but no one had the keys. So, he ordered that the locks be broken.

'There were innumerable items lying on top of each other under layers of dust and cobwebs. I put some people to work. I said: "Do an inventory and tell me what is useful and what is not." I warned them that I would do a third-party inspection, so they'd better give me a correct report. I said, "I will remove you from your jobs if you give me a wrong report."'

Then he learnt that a senior officer was blackmailing people regarding the report.

Awasthi told him: 'You are not working like a true professional,' and suspended him.

The officer had some connections in the media and fed journalists with stories against Awasthi. A leading English weekly wrote an article against him under the headline 'Most Expensive Chief Executive of India.' An air-conditioned Maruti 1000 that he had purchased with board approval for his commute to Thal from Trombay was the reason for this sobriquet.

Awasthi also suspended a very senior officer who had tried to forge his writing on a file. 'I always draw a circle around my remarks. This gentleman wrote "OK" or something, a very short word, near my signature. When I saw the file, I sensed the mischief. I called him and said, "Mister, this is not my writing." He said, "No, this is yours."'

Awasthi called his secretary and told him to bring other files with his remarks. Each file had encircled remarks. 'I suspended him citing "lack of confidence in the officer" as the reason.'

Awasthi held charge of RCF for a little more than a year, from February 1991 to March 1992, but his stint was very eventful.

He uncovered a big scam within a few months of taking charge. The catalyst in the nitric acid plant had corroded within a month or two of it being installed. The catalyst, coated with platinum, rhodium and palladium, has a normal life of three to four years. As a chemical engineer, Awasthi could not believe such an alloy would corrode so fast. There was a bank guarantee of ₹18 crore on the catalyst and it had been issued a certificate by a laboratory in New Jersey. It was the only accredited laboratory in the world that could certify that the catalyst met all the required criteria.

Awasthi sent a senior executive from RCF to New Jersey without informing anyone. He brought back a report from the laboratory stating that the certificate was fake. Awasthi told the finance director of RCF to encash the bank guarantee.

That caused panic in the company and a whole range of dirty tricks were rolled out to intimidate him. 'They went straight to the Prime Minister's Office (PMO). I was asked not to encash the bank guarantee. My wife called from Delhi to say someone had fired at our flat. The same night, a lady called her and said, "Your husband has married me; he is sleeping in my bedroom; he will leave you, so you take a divorce from him." But I did not budge and pursued the encashment. The bank manager tried to stall my move. I told him he would lose his job if I called the press and told them the full story. He transferred the money to RCF's account,' said Awasthi.

Awasthi was relieved of the additional charge of RCF in March 1992. PPCL had stabilized by then. P.V. Krishnaswamy, the Secretary in the Department of Fertilizers, and R.V. Gupta, the Additional Secretary in the department, were very happy with his work. Gupta was also the chairman of IFFCO at that time.

Both IFFCO and KRIBHCO were looking for managing directors. They exhorted Awasthi to apply for the posts. He did and was the first choice for both positions. KRIBHCO then had more money in its kitty. It looked more prosperous. People advised him to join KRIBHCO, but he chose IFFCO.

Explaining the rationale behind his choice, Awasthi said, 'I had gone to PPCL from IFFCO after spending ten years there. I was actively involved in its expansion and growth. So, my heart lay with IFFCO. Also, from 1988 onwards, it had fallen on difficult times. It was very agonizing for me. I was looking for the opportunity to return to IFFCO and revive it to its former glory.'

There was another reason as well. During Avdhani's tenure as managing director, a senior executive had been wrangling to be appointed as his successor. This executive lobbied with politicians and got the common marketing mechanism for IFFCO and KRIBHCO disbanded. The ostensible reason: this would create more jobs.

Political interference had ruined the work atmosphere at KRIBHCO and had badly, but not yet irretrievably, damaged the culture at IFFCO. Avdhani had quit in disgust, and several managing directors had followed in quick succession. Awasthi wanted to return to IFFCO, which he considered the mother organization of KRIBHCO, and set things right.

Awasthi's farewell from PPCL was a spectacular affair. The entire unit turned up to see him off. His open jeep was tethered to an elephant, which pulled it around the complex. People ran alongside it, chanting his name. His wife was with him.

Three decades after the event, Awasthi still looks visibly overwhelmed while narrating the scenes from his farewell party.

A hijack that wasn't

Awasthi was booked on the Patna–Lucknow–Delhi flight. There were several politicians in the plane—Sitaram Kesri, Ramdulari Sinha, Jagannath Mishra's son…there were others, too. When the plane left Lucknow, a person sprang up, claiming to have a chemical bomb in his hand. He said, 'Do as I say, otherwise I'll blow up the plane.'

Awasthi's wife shrieked in fear.

'Shut up,' the man shouted at her.

Airhostesses and stewards started pleading with the hijacker. They offered him water and other things, but he declined. 'No, I will not eat anything. Take the plane back to Lucknow.'

Awasthi whispered to Rekha in Hindi, 'This fellow looks like a fraud to me. I have half a mind to give him a tight slap and snatch his bomb.'

'Stop talking nonsense,' she replied.

The plane was taken back to Lucknow. Commandos surrounded the plane as soon as it landed. The hijacker asked for a meeting with Atal Bihari Vajpayee, who was an opposition leader then.

Jagannath Mishra's son said, 'I need to go to the toilet.'

The hijacker refused.

'I can't hold back. I'll dirty this place,' he pleaded.

'*Achcha, jao* [Okay, go],' the hijacker relented.

It was an Avro plane, which had an emergency exit in the bathroom. The man opened the door and signalled to the commandos to come in. One of the commandos, with similar build and height to his, donned his clothes and took his seat. In the meantime, a person dressed to look like Vajpayee from a distance appeared in view.

Rekha, extremely frightened, began twisting and turning in her seat. The commando, seated in the row behind Awasthi, whispered, 'Hold your wife. I'm going to shoot him.'

Awasthi held her hand firmly. The commando did not shoot; instead, he pounced on the hijacker and pinned him down. The bomb was a fake—made of flour.

This brought the curtain down on Awasthi's eventful stint at PPCL.

FOUR

YOU WIN SOME, YOU LOSE SOME

Awasthi took charge as managing director of IFFCO on 1 February 1993. Prime Minister P.V. Narasimha Rao and Finance Minister Manmohan Singh had begun opening up and liberalizing the Indian economy. Many old shibboleths were being cast aside. Several large business groups, long used to dictating terms in a protected market, found themselves unprepared to face the rising competition.

It was also a time of uncertainty and turmoil in IFFCO. Awasthi had joined PPCL from IFFCO in 1986. In the seven years between 1986 and 1993, IFFCO had had four chairmen and three managing directors.

The company had stopped growing and its credibility was being questioned. Awasthi was aware of everything, but he still chose to return as he was emotionally attached to IFFCO, it being a farmers' organization. He had been involved in its expansion for ten years, so he had been waiting for the opportunity to restore it to its former glory.

There were squabbles among the board members, and the management had become directionless. There was also a discernible lack of enthusiasm among the employees. As a result, the organization had stopped developing.

A board of directors meeting was held in the first week of March, a month after Awasthi took over as managing director. He presented the budget for 1993–1994 and informed the board that, for the first time,

IFFCO would pay income tax. Due to investment allowance and other tax-saving options, the company had not paid income tax till then.

Tiff at first board meeting

From the very outset, Awasthi had a clear vision of where he wanted to take the company and he was determined to get there, even if it meant he had to step on a few powerful toes.

'I had a tiff at my first board meeting. There was disagreement among the directors over manpower planning. The nominees of the financial institutions wanted an outside agency to do the manpower planning. I told them that I had already constituted a high-level committee of our own officers with an expert from outside for the purpose and we should wait for its recommendations before taking any action,' said Awasthi.

The outside agency was expensive. Awasthi's priority was to purge all non-essential expenses. In the same meeting, he got a resolution passed authorizing the management to prepay all foreign currency loans and those taken from financial institutions.

This would result in two major advantages—first, prepayment to financial institutions would remove their nominees from the board of directors. These nominees were interfering in the decision-making process.

'I told the board this was how I wanted to function,' he said.

Secondly, IFFCO was incurring huge losses on the repayment of foreign currency loans because of the volatility in exchange rates. Awasthi paid off all foreign currency loans in 1997. Till then, the company had incurred losses of ₹250 crore on these loans.

Awasthi's laser focus on costs drew his attention to the high demurrage charges IFFCO was paying at Kandla port. 'We import phosphoric acid for our Kandla plant, but due to the overcrowding of ships at Kandla port, we could not unload the acid within the time limit. Hence, we had to pay huge sums of money as demurrage charges,' he said.

The solution: Awasthi decided to build a jetty for IFFCO's liquid cargo. It took two and a half years to get all the necessary permissions. The jetty was completed in 1996 and started saving IFFCO significant sums of money. Later on, IFFCO built another jetty for solid cargoes. Now, the company unloads its cargoes in the middle of the sea and brings them to the plant on barges.

'I cut unnecessary expenses and started using those savings for the expansion of the organization,' said Awasthi.

Winning over the unions

Thereafter, the newly appointed managing director opened wage negotiations with the unions and the associations. The long-term wage settlement had been pending for a while. Earlier, the wage revision would be done every five years. IFFCO was established in 1967, and the first pay revision was for the period 1972–1976. Paul Pothen was the managing director at that time. The two wage revisions that followed—for 1977–1981 and 1982–1986—had been in dispute.

The unions and associations at the Kandla plant had accepted the revised pay scales but those at Kalol and Phulpur had been opposing it. This led to disputes that were decided by the National Tribunal. Aggrieved by the award of the National Tribunal, the union moved the Supreme Court. Awasthi resolved the disputes by taking everyone into confidence and started negotiations for the period starting 1977. This restored the confidence of the unions in the management. They withdrew the case from the Supreme Court, and it was agreed that, in the future, every legal matter would be settled with the management. They would move to the courts only as a last resort. This improved industrial relations in IFFCO and employees started to feel a sense of ownership towards the organization.

Awasthi also took several steps to improve working conditions at IFFCO and adopted international standards everywhere in the company. 'We started five-day weeks to allow employees to spend more time with their families. All offices were made no-smoking zones. Housing loan limits were raised, medical facilities were improved, and a high-level committee was constituted to draft a new promotion policy,' he said.

As the new managing director, he also wrote the Powers of Officers and simplified the procurement and contracting processes. All these changes automatized the company's systems and procedures.

Awasthi's management mantra

'When you go to any organization, you first figure out its weak spots and fix them. Then you make the foundation of the organization stronger and generate enthusiasm among the people there. After that, you solve the problems that the plants have. If a plant is being revived, you contribute to it intelligently. You plan for the expansion and implement it systematically. We started all these works in the first year itself,' said Awasthi, explaining the rationale behind his decisions.

As a result of these changes, IFFCO produced 1.36 lakh tonnes more in his first year as managing director—27.36 lakh tonnes compared to 26 lakh tonnes earlier, or about 5.2 per cent more—than its existing production capacity.

IFFCO was a co-promoter of Godavari Fertilizers, which makes complex fertilizers. The Government of Andhra Pradesh was its major shareholder. IFFCO held only 25 per cent of its shares. The company began incurring losses after the decontrol of DAP/NPK in 1992. Eighty per cent of its equity had been wiped out. IFFCO received a proposal to invest further in the company in order to revive it. 'We started considering the proposal very seriously,' said Awasthi.

Cross-currents of India's politics

Early in his tenure as managing director of IFFCO, Awasthi had two run-ins with Prime Minister P.V. Narasimha Rao. The first instance involved a sick sugar mill in Nandyal, Rao's parliamentary constituency. Pressure was brought to bear upon IFFCO to revive the sugar mill, which was weighed down by huge debts.

Awasthi was reluctant to wade into this as IFFCO had no domain expertise in the sugar sector. But IFFCO's chairman, P. Ramachandra Reddy, who hailed from Andhra Pradesh, was very close to Rao. He wanted to revive the mill.

Vijay Bhaskar Reddy was the Chief Minister of Andhra Pradesh at that time. Awasthi had to go and meet him many times along with the chairman. The chief minister was very hard of hearing. Once, he became very angry with Awasthi and shouted, 'Why don't you understand me?'

Awasthi shouted back, 'I will not waste IFFCO's money.'

This made Ramachandra Reddy very nervous. He took Awasthi out and said, 'What are you doing? Don't do this.'

Then Awasthi suggested that IFFCO would provide a loan to revive the sugar mill. They accepted this suggestion. 'We gave a loan of ₹4 crore to that sugar mill in 1994, and got the money back in 2003,' said Awasthi with a shrug and a wry smile.

Around the same time, a person claiming to be close to Narasimha Rao visited Awasthi at the IFFCO office in Nehru Place. This individual had official security cover. This created quite a scene at IFFCO's office—it was a sight to behold!

'The person asked me to deposit ₹100 crore in a certain bank. I said, "If the provisions of my organization permit it then I will have no objection to depositing the money. We have only A category banks on our panel, and we deposit our money with those banks only." The recommended bank was not on our panel,' recalls Awasthi.

He discussed the idea with M.K. Tandon, who was then IFFCO's finance director. He said it would be very risky to oblige the person. Awasthi was also against the idea.

He told the person, 'This will not be possible.'

The person was obviously not used to being refused. 'What's wrong with this proposal?' this individual demanded to know. 'You have to take your money from one bank and deposit it in another bank. What is illegal in it?'

'You are right, but the rules of my organization do not permit me to do this.'

This person tried many different arguments, but Awasthi kept saying, with folded hands, that it would not be possible. The VIP went away very angry. Later the same day, there was a call from the PMO saying, 'It was such a small thing; yet you could not do it.'

'Sir, I wish I could do that, but I am bound by the rules of my organization. I am sorry that I disappointed you. I will readily do something for you or for anyone if my organization permits.

The caller said "Okay" curtly and hung up,' Awasthi shared.

Awasthi has had to face many such awkward situations over the last three decades, but he has never compromised the interests of IFFCO or of farmers.

A step towards full autonomy

IFFCO's Chairman Ramachandra Reddy died suddenly on 12 October 1995. At that time, the board of directors used to be constituted for three years and the chairman's tenure was co-terminus with that of the board. Reddy had completed one term as chairman and had been re-elected to the post in May 1995.

The government nominated D.P. Yadav in his place on the board of IFFCO. Yadav was a Lok Sabha MP from Bihar and had a deep understanding of Indian agriculture. The tradition in IFFCO until that time was that the director nominated by the government was elected as the chairman, so Yadav was elected interim chairman in December 1995 for the remainder of Reddy's tenure.

In January 1997, the government recalled Yadav and nominated Major General Samay Ram in his place. The IFFCO board didn't like this unilateral decision take by the government. It decided to do away with the convention of electing the government nominee as the chairman. The board then took a collective decision that from then on it would only elect someone from the field of cooperatives as chairman.

So, no member of the board proposed the name of Major General Ram. Instead, Surinder Jakhar was unanimously elected as chairman. Sis Ram Ola was the Union Minister of State for Chemicals and Fertilizers (Independent Charge) at that time. He thought Awasthi had manipulated the process to have Jakhar elected.

'I went and explained to him that IFFCO was a cooperative society and its members had unanimously decided that from then on they would only elect a person active in the cooperative movement as its chairman,' said Awasthi.

It was the beginning of a new era in the history of IFFCO, and this took it a step closer towards becoming 'wholly owned by cooperatives'. This new tradition started with the 242nd meeting of the board of directors on 22 January 1997.

'It was a proud occasion for IFFCO, and I am happy that I was part of it,' he said.

Some years later, in 1999, when Atal Bihari Vajpayee was the Prime Minister of India, Awasthi got a call from the PMO. Shakti Sinha, Vajpayee's Private Secretary, was on the line. He told Awasthi that the Prime Minister wanted him to vote for a particular candidate in the election for the chairmanship of KRIBHCO. In those days, many IFFCO and KRIBHCO directors sat on each other's boards.

Awasthi said, 'I have already given my word to someone else.' He had committed his support to Chandrapal Singh Yadav, who was a big name in the cooperative world.

After about an hour, Sinha called back. 'The prime minister said it's okay,' he said.

'This is a beautiful memory. I was touched by Atal-ji's gesture,' said Awasthi.

This incident has become part of the fertilizer industry and cooperative sector folklore. Government nominees made up 50 per cent of the strength of the KRIBHCO board. They had all been directed to vote for the other candidate, but Awasthi's backing saw Yadav through.

The cooperative movement by definition is a democratic one. But government control was standing this principle on its head. The chairmen of IFFCO, KRIBHCO, National Agricultural Cooperative Marketing Federation (NAFED) and other multi-state cooperatives used to be government nominees. That was the convention, because the government was the largest shareholder. There were many occasions when the government removed and appointed chairmen at its will, completely disregarding the principles of democracy.

It was Awasthi who inspired cooperatives to stand up for this cooperative principle of democracy and elect chairmen of their own choice, first in IFFCO, and then in other multi-state cooperatives in the country, said Yadav. 'It was exceptional on his part to do what he did,' he continues. 'People get frightened at the mere mention of the PMO. But here was someone who stood his ground against the direction of the prime minister. It was indeed a big deal.'

In the NAFED election, too, the cooperatives wrested back control from the government and elected their own representative as chairman.

'We all recognize and admire Awasthi's dedication towards the cooperative movement in India,' said a senior cooperator with a hearty laugh.

Expansion plans

Awasthi embarked on expanding the capacity of his plants from his first year as the managing director of IFFCO. Kalol is considered the company's mother plant. There, the pressure of gas supply had reduced. Awasthi said, 'Let's fire naphtha and have a pre-reformer.' A pre-reformer converts naphtha into gas. 'Thus, we increased the production capacity of the Kalol plant,' he said.

The plan for expanding the Aonla plant was already in the works when Awasthi joined IFFCO. 'We re-evaluated it and brought its budget down from ₹1,100 crore to ₹960 crore,' said Awasthi. Government approvals for the expansion of the Aonla plant came in September 1993.

Awasthi devised a clever strategy to reduce the cost of the Aonla expansion. NFL was expanding its Vijaipur plant at that time. Both receive gas from the HVJ pipeline; both use the same technology, and both were commissioned around the same time. So, he talked to the government and got permission to start both projects together.

'This allowed us to spend relatively less on consultants and equipment. With the savings we made, we kept dual feedstock in Aonla so we could switch to naphtha in case of any problem with the supply of gas,' he said, adding, 'The next year (1994) we started the expansion of the Phulpur plant and began preparations for setting up an ammonia–urea complex at Nellore in Andhra Pradesh. We also started exploring the possibility of setting up a complex fertilizer plant in West Asia.'

IFFCO had tried to set up a complex fertilizer plant in Iran, but this effort did not succeed. Then it expanded its phosphoric acid production capacity in Senegal in West Africa.

'In 1994, we increased the number of general managers and joint general managers in IFFCO because the plants were being expanded. The Aonla expansion had already started and the Phulpur expansion was about to begin. To reduce the cost of the Phulpur expansion and complete the project on time, we came up with a new approach,' he said.

The orders for long delivery items (equipment and machinery that take more than forty-eight months to deliver) that were placed for the Aonla expansion were also placed for Phulpur. This way, the technology for the Aonla expansion was utilized for Phulpur, too, and both expansion projects were completed in the shortest possible time—in forty-two months and thirty-two months, respectively.

These were records in the fertilizer industry—Oswal Chemicals had taken forty-five months, Nagarjuna Fertilizers forty-seven months, National Fertilizers forty-nine months, Chambal Fertilizers fifty-two months and Tata Fertilizers fifty-three months for similar projects. IFFCO managed this feat beating stiff odds, and Awasthi doesn't shy away from giving credit where it's due.

'I am saying this emphatically: the IFFCO board had a big role in this. They are very sincere and have a highly positive outlook. They ask questions as they should, but when they are convinced that a decision is in the interest of the company, they do not hesitate to give their consent and offer all cooperation,' he said.

Paul Pothen was a nominated member on the board at that time and he provided able guidance to the IFFCO management (led by Awasthi) through the many crises it had to weather during the expansion phase.

Out-of-the-box solutions save the day

Awasthi's problem-solving skills and out-of-the-box thinking came to the fore when these plants were being expanded. IFFCO had placed the order for the high temperature and low temperature converter on Bharat Heavy Plates and Vessels (BHPV). The delivery of the converter, which is 60–70 metres long and 5–7 metres wide, was getting delayed because of worker unrest at the vendor's end. The converter was lying there in two pieces; the welding was yet to be done.

Awasthi took the bold call to ferry the converter from Visakhapatnam in two pieces to the site in Aonla and weld it on-site. It was a very difficult task, made all the more challenging by the fact that the monsoon was about to break. The IFFCO managing director decided on a multimodal transport solution, decades before the concept became popular. The converter would be transported from BHPV's works in Visakhapatnam to Kandla by sea, and from there to Aonla by road.

The contractor was given fifteen days for the transportation. Because of this, the cost of transportation would be a little more than the budgeted amount, but most importantly, the converter would be delivered on time. Then, bad weather struck. The marketing team did an exceptional job at that time. Wherever they encountered problems, they organized local people and paved the way for the movement of the converter—they repaired the roads, strengthened the bridges, crossed different high points and brought the equipment to Aonla on time.

Similarly, there was unrest at Lloyd Steel, on which IFFCO had placed an order for some critical items. 'We negotiated with them, and it was decided that we would pay for the purchase of their materials. We sent senior executives from our technical and finance departments to oversee the work there. We were given a separate space at Lloyd Steel where our workers and welders completed the work,' said Awasthi.

Meanwhile, there was a flood in Bharatpur, Rajasthan, where some other equipment was being made. 'We immediately sent our team, lifted the equipment and brought it to Aonla. We have always remained alert. We solved all the problems promptly and completed the project on time,' he said.

The Aonla project was scheduled to be completed on 1 January 1997, but IFFCO managed to do it by 13 December 1996. IFFCO also saved ₹5 crore. It was the fastest project to be completed at that time.

An ustad who could make problems vanish

The Aonla project brought along with it some interesting stories, said N.K. Kedia, General Manager, Planning and Development, IFFCO, and now Chairman, IFFCO-Tokio Insurance Services (ITIS), the microinsurance arm of IFFCO-Tokio General Insurance. 'We used to call Dr Awasthi "Ustad" among ourselves. He has the unique ability to recognize who can do what. So, he always places the right person in the right place for the right job. Whenever we had any problem with respect to the organization or at a personal level, he was always there.'

Awasthi is a good listener, and he has a positive attitude. So, he was ideally suited for the role.

'But there was one bad thing also. If he did not like someone, then he did not like that person. There would have to be a good reason for that, though. He is still like that,' said Kedia.

Standing his ground for India

Kedia recalls an incident when he was posted in the head office of Snamprogetti in Milan. There was some confusion over who would be chosen to supply the carbon dioxide compressor for the urea plant. Some people wanted the contract to go to a certain multinational company.

One day before the bids were to be opened, an executive from the consultant's side told Kedia, 'We want this order.'

'We will open the bids tomorrow. Let's see what happens,' Kedia replied.

When the bids were opened, the company the foreign executive had been backing was L4 (fourth lowest bidder). An Indian company was the L1 (lowest) bidder.

That person again came and said, 'We want this order at any cost. Remember one thing: if this does not happen, then your Managing

Director (MD) will change.' He dropped the name of a very big officer in the Department of Fertilizers in the Government of India.

Kedia telephoned Awasthi and told him everything. 'He told me to get the evaluation of the bids done quickly and come to India. I flew back to India with the detailed evaluation.'

Normally it takes ten to fifteen weeks from the date of opening the bids to place the final order. Awasthi arranged for a special board meeting where the L1 bidder was selected and the order was placed. The acceptance of the bidder was also put on record. Everything happened in the span of six weeks.

The foreign executive came to India to enquire about the order, certain that the process was still on. He was taken aback when he was told that the order had already been placed. He tried to pull strings in favour of the vendor he was backing.

'We were called to the ministry for clarifications,' said Kedia.

Awasthi sent him there with all the papers and explained everything to the competent authority. There was no confusion after that.

This ability to counteract opposition has been a hallmark of Awasthi's long tenure as managing director of IFFCO. He always tries to give maximum orders to Indian companies, especially to public sector units, and enjoys a wonderful rapport with them. They give IFFCO good prices and they go out of their way to make deliveries on time.

This is part of Awasthi's philosophy of maintaining good relations with government departments.

'The year 1996 was very satisfying for me,' Awasthi said.

First Asian president of IFA

The year 1997 was full of milestones, achievements and at least one rude shock. He was elected the president of the International Fertilizer Association (IFA), becoming the first Asian in the association's eighty-year history to be elected to that position.

IFA had, till then, been dominated by fertilizer industry leaders from the US and Europe. But Awasthi was getting noticed by influential people even before he became managing director of IFFCO.

Luc Maene, who served for many years as director general of IFA, said, 'I met Awasthi when he was with PPCL. I used to tell everyone, "PPCL is such a small company. This man should do something more." He had a vision. He was saying things I did not hear elsewhere in the industry.'

When Maene joined IFA, he decided to get people from outside the US and Europe to become members of its board and, eventually, the chairman of IFA. Awasthi stood out among the potential candidates.

The IFA has a system whereby one serves as vice president, senior vice president and then becomes chairman—all over a period of six years.

'I groomed Awasthi to take over. He was an excellent choice,' said Maene, adding, 'He's also a very charismatic person. So, I was very happy grooming him and he made an excellent chairman.'

Awasthi also had the advantage of being from the cooperative sector, which is somewhere between the public and the private sectors. So, he was acceptable to all—a unanimous choice.

Awasthi started many new traditions at IFA. The chief executive of IFA used to be called the 'executive secretary.' He had it changed to 'director general.' He also started the tradition of having a vegetarian section on the menu at conferences. Earlier, participants had to pay extra to bring their spouses with them; Awasthi said, 'No, spouses' entry should be complimentary.' The participation fee was increased a little, and spouses were accommodated within that.

Reflecting its American–European heritage, IFA had a tradition of black-tie dinners. 'I said, 'What is this black-tie dinner?' Today we do not live in a strictly formal atmosphere. So, let's make it smart-casual. We should be smartly dressed, not officially dressed,' he said.

All these new traditions continue even today at IFA. Later, following in his boss's footsteps, Rakesh Kapur, IFFCO's joint managing director, also became the chairman of both IFA and the Fertilizer Association of India (FAI).

Ajay Shriram, Chairman and Senior Managing Director, DCM Shriram, the company where Awasthi began his professional life, considers him a friend as well as a competitor. He has no hesitation in saying, 'Awasthi planted the flag of the Indian fertilizer industry in the international fertilizer fraternity along with Pratap Narayan, the director general of FAI.'

Shriram doesn't remember exactly when, but said Awasthi also started hosting an 'IFFCO Evening' at IFA conferences. 'Once he hosted us on a boat in Istanbul. There were about 250 people on board and we were taken on a two-and-a-half-hour-long cruise. There was a band playing and singers were singing. Fantastic food was being served. The atmosphere was really good. It was very relaxing, and it was a place to get to know the who's who of the fertilizer world,' he recalls.

'It's a matter of great pride for both me and IFFCO—today, if you go to IFA conferences, you will find that they are such wonderful platforms for both professional interactions and social bonhomie,' said Awasthi.

Before this, Awasthi had been elected chairman of FAI, the industry body representing the country's fertilizer sector, in 1994.

There, too, he had brought about several changes in its culture; the chief executive used to be called 'executive director'. Awasthi changed that to 'director general.' He also started the tradition of employees bringing spouses to the conference.

'Wherever I have gone, I have tried to introduce family values that everyone likes,' he said.

More importantly, he took FAI to the world bodies of the fertilizer industry. As a result, India now figures prominently on the world fertilizer scene. If there is any new development in the industry, the Indian fertilizer sector immediately comes to know of it; it can straight away make those changes.

'People are not shy to share technology with us. They are not shy to set up JVs with us. We did everything we could do on the industry side, but we could not get the changes made on the government side, which could have been more pragmatic and suited to the requirements of the industry and the farmers of our country,' said Awasthi with a tinge of sadness.

A bolt from the blue

The year 1997 was shaping up to be a perfect one for Awasthi. The expansion of the Aonla and Kalol plants had been completed. The Phulpur expansion was nearing completion, the expansion of Kandla and Senegal were about to begin.

It came as a rude shock when, on 30 September that year, an income tax raid was carried out on Awasthi and ten senior executives of IFFCO. The houses of his secretary, R.K. Chawla, and his elder sister, Vidya Pandey, were also raided.

Nothing significant was recovered in those raids. 'They found some ten-fifteen thousand rupees in cash in my house. All our lockers were opened. Nothing was found which was undeclared or illegal. The result of the raid was that the Income Tax Department returned ₹8,000 to me on my ten years' income,' said Awasthi.

But the raid left a scar on his wife Rekha's psyche. There were some very personal letters from the early days of their marriage that Rekha had preserved. The Income Tax Department sleuths opened those letters and read them. She found this very distressing. It hurt her so much that after the raid she burnt all the letters and consecrated the ashes in the Yamuna.

But Awasthi did not take this raid as a personal affront. 'In a democracy people have the right to seek whatever information they want about anyone. I told my wife that we should not feel bad about it. It is part of public life. I have a place in public life, and people want to know about me. We should have no objection to this. But for my wife that incident was a matter of grave humiliation. The house of my elder sister, who was very old, was also raided. Her entire lawn was dug up to see if gold was buried there. These are the two incidents that were hurtful; otherwise, I have no complaints,' he said.

Then, he adds after a moment's silence, 'It's always your own people who dishonour you. This happens in our country, and this has happened to me time and again. But this has never deterred me from doing what I want to do. I have never compromised with my principles either out of fear or pressure. For me, my organization is always paramount. There can never be any compromise on that.'

Philosophy of life

The raid highlighted the philosophies Awasthi lives by. 'I do not live in a way that I look unnecessarily humble. I have been like this since my childhood. I might not have anything, but I walk as if I have the whole world with me. Because I have confidence in myself, I believe my shoulders are strong enough to bear any responsibility. I have confidence in my mind, I have faith in my heart, and I trust God. Since I have taken the right path, I will definitely succeed. I never think of failure, and I'm not afraid of anything,' he said, explaining how he maintains his equanimity in the midst of the turbulence he sometimes has to face.

'Secondly, I do not consider anyone bad. If someone does anything bad to me then I think he must have done it under some compulsion. I have never looked back to find out who has done what to me. If anyone supports me somewhere, then I try to repay his favour as soon as possible. But if anyone tries to hurt me, then I overlook it because sorrow is a state of mind. If I overlook it, then there is no sorrow. I always keep in mind what the great poet Kabir had said: *Lambi maar Kabir ki, chit se diya utar* [You banish from the heart, this is the surest remedy].'

Expansion in West Asia: ammonia–urea complex in Oman

In July 1994, the Government of India and the Sultanate of Oman signed a memorandum of understanding (MOU) to set up a commercially viable, world-class ammonia–urea complex in Oman. RCF and KRIBHCO on the Indian side, and the Oman Oil Company on the Omani side were the sponsors of the project.

The three sponsors entered into a JV agreement to set up a new company called Oman India Fertilizer Company (OMIFCO), in which the Oman Oil Company would hold a 50 per cent stake and RCF and KRIBHCO would own 25 per cent each. It was agreed between the three sponsors that the Oman Oil Company would supply gas to the project at a fixed price and RCF and KRIBHCO would buy the entire production of urea at the going international price.

In September 1998, the Indian government proposed that IFFCO join this JV as an equal partner of RCF and KRIBHCO because it had experience in setting up overseas projects.

Awasthi took this proposal to the board. Most of the directors were against it. The two joint secretaries in the Department of Fertilizers were also not in favour of investing in OMIFCO. But Awasthi took the stand that this project was important for fertilizer supply and food security in the country and so ought to be pursued.

The common refrain of the naysayers was, 'Oman doesn't have enough gas.' Also, the price of oil in the international market had crashed to $9 per barrel; there had also been a sharp fall in the prices of ammonia and urea; so, there was a general apprehension that this project would not be successful.

The price of urea had also fallen from $200 per tonne to $80 per tonne between 1994 and 1998, when the project was conceived. The banks that were financing the project thought this would reduce the cash flows of the company and began to voice doubts about the viability of the project.

They put very tough conditions—like seeking a sovereign guarantee from the Indian government—for advancing loans.

There was a heated debate about this project in Parliament. It was argued that this project was not practical. It was a stalemate—the Government of India refused to give a sovereign guarantee, and the banks refused to budge from their stand without the security of this assurance.

There seemed to be no easy route out of this impasse. But Awasthi was steadfast in his views that 'this project is very important for the country'. He proposed that the Government of India should buy all the urea produced by OMIFCO at a predetermined price instead of the international price.

The government agreed to this, and IFFCO undertook to buy all the ammonia that would be produced. This brought a measure of certitude to the cash flows of the JV and served to reassure the skittish bankers that their loans would be serviced without too much risk.

Awasthi also worked on the project, reduced its cost, negotiated with the banks on how the lending would happen and negotiated with the Government of Oman on the long-term pricing of urea. He also negotiated the ammonia prices based on international prices.

'Though the initial MoU was signed in 1994, the project was hanging in the balance till IFFCO joined it in 1998. Since the capital cost of the project was very high, KRIBHCO and RCF felt the need to bring in another partner,' said Birinder Singh, Director, Corporate Services, IFFCO, who was actively involved in the Oman project as an IFFCO representative.

'Dr Awasthi analysed the project and felt the cost of $1.106 billion was too high. He negotiated with Snamprogetti and Technip-Coflexip, the technology suppliers, and managed to reduce the cost by doing away with some equipment that he considered redundant. The cost was reduced to $969 million, and the production capacity increased from 14.52 lakh tonnes to 16.52 lakh tonnes,' said Birinder Singh, adding that Awasthi's intervention significantly increased the commercial viability of the project.

A global organization, CRU International Limited, forecasts urea prices in the international market. Its estimate of urea prices in the international market for the next fifteen years was largely in line with the projections that Awasthi's team had made. 'This, it was thought, would provide the government with a measure of comfort,' said Manish Gupta, Director, Joint Venture & Strategy Division, IFFCO, a former Indian Revenue Service officer, who was Deputy Secretary in the Department of Fertilizers when the project was being negotiated.

'There were discussions in the ministry on whether the prices of urea fixed for fifteen years were fair and whether the government should buy urea from the Oman project at these predetermined prices. At that time, the price of urea in the international market was $80 per tonne.'

The government was being asked to pay $150 per tonne in the first year. After that, it was $140, then it was $130, with prices gradually decreasing every year.

'It is not easy in the government to buy something worth $80 for $150. The finance ministry and the Planning Commission were totally against this project. The commerce ministry was also not in favour. The Department of Fertilizers was rooting for the project because the country needed urea. The Ministry of External Affairs wanted the project to go ahead because Oman and India had very good diplomatic relations. From 1999 to 2002, these differences continued. No one believed that this project would ever start,' said Gupta.

Then confusion arose about ammonia. Some surplus ammonia was being produced. Though it was only a small quantity, the lenders said there should be some arrangement to sell the surplus ammonia too. Awasthi resolved this problem by saying: 'IFFCO will buy the surplus ammonia.'

It was decided that IFFCO would pay a fixed price of $100 per tonne. IFFCO was ready to commit to the offtake for fifteen years, but the contract was signed for ten years only. At that time, the lenders and the Oman Oil Company thought they might get more than $100 in the international market.

Awasthi said, 'Okay, if someone gives you more than $100, then you sell your ammonia to them.' They tried in the international market, but no one was ready to pay more than $100. That's how the issue of ammonia was also resolved.

But IFFCO and KRIBHCO, government-controlled companies, needed approvals before they could invest in OMIFCO. And that kept being delayed on one pretext or the other.

'One day, suddenly, we were told this project would be discussed at the Cabinet meeting the next day. A note was immediately prepared and presented to the Cabinet. Vajpayee first asked everyone to present their arguments. The Ministry of Finance, Ministry of Commerce, and Planning Commission opposed the project. Jaswant Singh, who was the foreign minister, said all the things that had been said in opposition to the project were about investment. But he said that considering the diplomatic benefits that India would get from this project, the investment was justified. 'The prime minister listened to everyone silently and said two words at the end: "Project approved,"' recalls Gupta.

The matter had been pending for eight years. No one knew whether the project would ever be cleared. One night, the call came, and the next morning, the project was approved. The file was finally closed.

IFFCO could now join the project as an equal partner of KRIBHCO and RCF.

But there was another twist in the tale. At this point, RCF decided to pull out of the project stating that its financials were still very weak.

Awasthi again came to the rescue of the project, committing to buy RCF's share in the project. After some negotiations, it was decided that the Oman Oil Company would continue to hold 50 per cent in the JV, while IFFCO and KRIBHCO would hold 25 per cent each.

'In 2002, we formally joined the project,' said Birinder Singh. 'By then, it had finally reached a stage where it could be started. The zero date of the project was 15 August 2002.'

Awasthi also contributed significantly to the construction of the project. Under his guidance, the project was completed on time and within budget. It turned out to be a wonderful plant that reached 100 per cent capacity utilization within fifteen days, against the norm of running plants at 85–90 per cent capacity in the first year.

When commercial production started in 2005, the prices of urea and ammonia had risen again in the international market—to much higher levels than their predetermined prices. This enabled the Government of India to save billions of dollars in subsidies—some estimates put the figure at ₹22,300 crore. The sponsors of the project also earned very good profits.

Expansion of existing plants

In his initial years as managing director of IFFCO, Awasthi concentrated on expanding existing plants rather than on greenfield projects.

He explains, 'We had tried setting up new plants, but those efforts were not successful. In 1995, we bought 3,000 acres of land in Nellore in Andhra Pradesh to set up an ammonia–urea complex. Our then chairman, Ramachandra Reddy, was from Nellore. The project had received permission in the first phase, but in the second phase it could not get the permission because it was naphtha based. The government had decided not to have naphtha-based plants in the country.'

IFFCO had also tried to set up a urea plant in the Northeast because gas is available there, but this, too, could not progress beyond the first phase. The company also had plans to set up a complex fertilizer plant in Iran, but this did not take off.

'There are many advantages associated with the expansion of existing plants,' said Awasthi with wisdom born of experience. 'You save both on cost and time as the basic infrastructure and manpower are already available in the plant.'

IFFCO expanded four plants in four and a half years. These endeavours earned profuse praise. The Additional Secretary of the Department of Programme Implementation wrote to Awasthi saying, 'Please accept my heartiest congratulations [...] The members of the team under your leadership have done a commendable job. When a large number of projects in many sectors are running behind schedule, it is a matter of satisfaction that at least some projects are completed even ahead of schedule [...] We would like to carry out an ex-post facto evaluation of the three projects completed ahead of schedule. These case studies would be quite educative and may be used in training programmes. The project managers would get an idea of how to complete major projects on schedule.'

While the Kandla plant was being expanded in 1998, Awasthi also bought 4.26 acres of land in Sector 29 in Gurgaon, where he planned to build IFFCO's new head office. However, this plan was subsequently shelved and the IFFCO Twin Towers were built in Sector 29, Gurgaon.

Call of duty: cyclone relief in Kandla

IFFCO had just completed the expansion of its plants when a tsunami-like cyclone struck Kandla on 9 June 1998. It was the worst calamity that the Kutch region had suffered in the last hundred years. The IFFCO plant was submerged in 3–4 feet of seawater.

'We put our disaster management plan into action as soon as we received information about the cyclone. The plant was shut down in advance. There was no loss of human life at our plant. We had taken all our ships away, but the adjoining government jetty came and hit our dolphin. We had to get it repaired at a cost of about ₹5 crore,' said Awasthi.

IFFCO immediately provided money to the collectorate for food and medical aid. There was total disruption of power supply from the Gujarat Electricity Board. The plant could resume production partially with its own generators after a week. It took nearly a month for normalcy to return.

Touching lives

Santosh Kumari is a 'model farmer' in Ghatampur Kheda. Until a few years ago, she struggled to put together two square meals for herself and her two sons. She eked out a miserable existence on her tiny plot of farmland.

Her elder son learnt about modern farming techniques at a kisan mela organized by IFFCO and said they should install a submersible pump for irrigation.

'We do not have that kind of money. How can we buy a submersible pump?' said Santosh Kumari.

'Don't worry. You will learn how it can happen,' he replied and took Santosh Kumari to attend IFFCO melas to learn about the benefits of growing vegetables and other cash crops.

They started with mustard and turmeric crops and saved some money. With their small saving and a small loan from a bank, they installed a submersible pump to improve the irrigation of their farm. Her husband was called back from the city where he had gone to earn a living, and together, they worked hard under IFFCO's guidance and managed to transform their lives.

'When we repaid the loan, the bank gave us another loan for a flour mill. Now we also have a spice grinder. IFFCO taught us about vermicompost. That has also given us good profits. There have been days when we sold vegetables worth ₹4,000 to ₹5,000 on a single day. MD Sahab [Awasthi] has called me many times and given me awards. I can't thank God enough for his grace. It has been unbelievable. May he bestow the same fortune on everyone,' she gushes.

Her younger son adds, 'What was remarkable was that IFFCO never left us in the lurch. Its executives kept coming back to provide timely support and guidance. We save ₹1 lakh to ₹2 lakh every year. Then, we earn additional incomes from the flour mill and the spice grinder. Now we understand what progress is.'

There are scores of such families that have been touched by Awasthi's outreach programmes. With minor variations, their stories follow the same linear plot—from despair and misery to a life of hope and relative prosperity.

This is a key area where Awasthi's corporate trajectory differs from that of many of his corporate peers—his uncanny knack of touching people's lives and bringing about material improvement.

A visionary and a leader

Chandrapal Singh Yadav, chairman of KRIBHCO, has worked closely with Awasthi for almost a quarter of a century and has observed him closely. 'He is a visionary and a leader,' he said. 'I have seen the transformation of IFFCO over the last twenty-five years. IFFCO was still limited in scale when he took charge. Today, it is the largest fertilizer cooperative in the world. It has JVs across the world. Every farmer in the country knows about IFFCO and has complete faith in its products.'

In the period from 1993 to 2000—the first phase of expansion under Awasthi—IFFCO's fertilizer production increased from 27.36 lakh tonnes to 52.76 lakh tonnes.

IFFCO was now strong and prosperous enough for a quantum leap.

'His technical competence, his ability to take quick decisions, and his art of carrying everyone along are qualities that you rarely find in a single person. And he is a good-natured, honest man. He enjoys helping people. I don't know of any cooperative member who has gone to him with his problems and returned disappointed,' said Yadav.

P.S. Gahlaut, managing director of Indian Potash Limited (IPL), who is himself a fertilizer industry legend, adds, 'Farmers, IFFCO and the nation—these are the three cornerstones of his vision. Today, IFFCO is a respected name in the global fertilizer industry and Awasthi is a credible name in the global fertilizer fraternity.'

Top: With Prime Minister Narendra Modi, at 7 Lok Kalyan Marg (PM's official residence) (2014)

Centre: With Union Home and Cooperation Minister, Amit Shah

Bottom: With Mansukh Mandaviya, Union Minister for Chemicals and Fertilizers, and Dileep Sanghani, IFFCO Chairman, while visiting the Nano Plant at Aonla (left to right)

Top: Mansukh Mandaviya, Union Minister for Chemicals and Fertilizers, inaugurating the IFFCO Nano Plant at Aonla

Bottom: With former Prime Minister of India, P.V. Narasimha Rao

Top: With former President of India, Shankar Dayal Sharma (1996)

Bottom: With former Prime Minister of India, I.K. Gujral

Top: With former Deputy Prime Minister of India, L.K. Advani

Bottom: Keshubhai Patel, S.S. Barnala and L.K. Advani inaugurating the new plant at Kalol

Top: With former Union Minister, Suresh Prabhu

Bottom: Sharad Pawar, former Union Agriculture Minister with awardee Vidyasagar Nautiyal and writer Namvar Singh at the Shrilal Shukla Smriti IFFCO Sahitya Samman Ceremony

Top: With former Lok Sabha Speaker, Somnath Chatterjee (2009)

Bottom: With Dr Karan Singh (2010)

Top: Awasthi being felicitated by former President of India, Pratibha Devi Singh Patil, for his outstanding contribution to the field of art and culture at Vigyan Bhawan, New Delhi (2011)

Bottom: With former President of India, Pranab Mukherjee, at the Rashtrapati Bhawan (2012)

Top: With former President of India, Dr A.P.J. Abdul Kalam

Bottom: With Nobel Peace Prize winner Desmond M. Tutu (2007)

Top: Paul Pothen addressing IFFCO employees on the new year (at the Nehru Place Head Office building in New Delhi) (1977)

Bottom: At PPCL's Saladipura mines (1987)

Top: Worshipping at IFFCO's Kandla Temple (1993)

Bottom: Awasthi inspecting a construction site at IFFCO's Aonla plant (1996)

Top: Visiting the Paradeep plant during the Golden Jubilee celebrations (2017)

Bottom: At the bhoomi pujan at IFFCO's Aonla plant expansion site (1993)

Top: Visiting IFFCO's Kandla plant (1993)

Bottom: With the Japanese OCOF team at the Aonla site (1984)

Top: With former president of the Federation of Indian Chambers of Commerce & Industry and Shriram Group promoter Charat Ram (1998)

Bottom: With Pranab Mukherjee, the then Finance Minister, at the inauguration of IFFCO farmer's service centre in West Bengal

Top: With Pratap Narayan, veteran bureaucrat and former Director General of the Fertilizer Association of India (1992)

Bottom: With his mentor Paul Pothen (second from right) (1981)

Top: In Dakar during the visit of S.S Barnala, the then Minister for Chemicals and Fertilizers, to ICS Senegal (1998)

Bottom: Signing of the MoU between IFFCO and Tokio Marine and Nichido Fire Insurance Company Ltd

Top: IFFCO and Mitsubishi Corporation signing an MoU at IFFCO Sadan (2015)

Bottom: Signing an agreement with Oswal (2005)

Top: Former Speaker of Lok Sabha Meira Kumar at an IFFCO function (2012)

Bottom: With IFFCO board members at Paradeep (2010)

Top: Visiting the control room of PPCL's Amjhore single super phosphate plant

Bottom: Ropeway construction at PPCL's Durmala mines, near Mussoorie

Top: Interacting with cooperators during farmers and cooperators' meet at S.K. Memorial Hall, Patna (2017)

Bottom: Female farmers taking a selfie with Awasthi during the Golden Jubilee celebrations at the Khatu Shyamji Temple, Rajasthan (2017)

Top: Jagannath Temple at IFFCO's Paradeep unit, a project very close to Awasthi's heart

Centre: With former Union Minister Ravi Shankar Prasad (2015)

Bottom: Visiting IFFCO's Aonla plant (2018)

Top: Inaugurating the Oman India Fertilizer Company in Oman with the then Union Minister of Chemicals and Fertilizers, Ram Vilas Paswan

Centre: Awasthi (extreme right) signing an agreement in the presence of the then Prime Minister of India, Dr Manmohan Singh, and Russian President, Vladimir Putin

Bottom: With Luc Maene, former Director General, IFA

Top: With Sunil Bharti Mittal, founder and chairperson of Bharti Enterprises

Bottom: Omar al-Razzaz, Prime Minister of Jordan along with Dr P.S. Gahlaut, MD, IPL; Dr Mohammad Thneibat, Chairman, JPMC; U.S. Awasthi; and Manish Gupta (right to left)

Top: Interacting with the King of Jordan, His Majesty Abdullah II bin Al-Hussein (2009)

Bottom: Signing an agreement with Jordan

Top: With Dr Haldor Topsøe at an ammonia plant

Bottom: Announcing the commercial launch of IFFCO nano-urea at the 50th Annual General Meeting (2021)

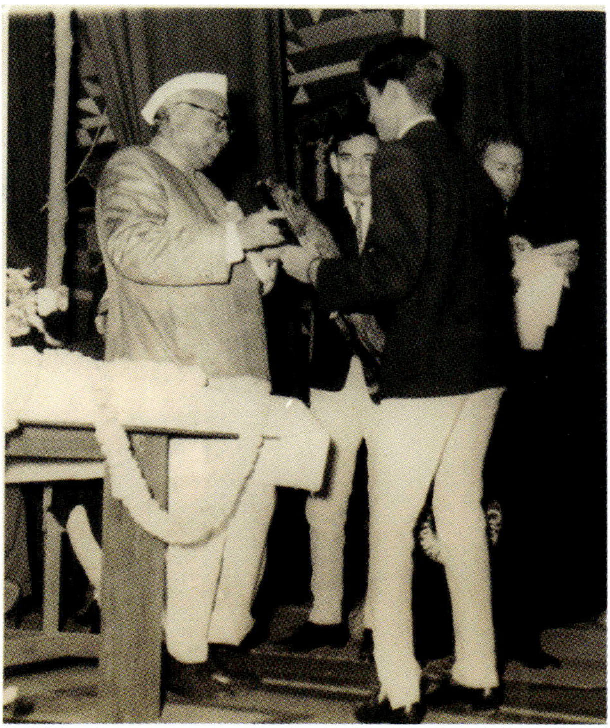

Top: Awasthi monitoring relief work for earthquake victims in Bhuj (2001)

Bottom: Awasthi receiving an award from Babu Jagjivan Ram at BHU (1964)

Top: Awasthi receiving the Uttar Pradesh Gaurav Award presented by the Society for Environment & Agriculture Advancement from the then Governor of Uttar Pradesh, Motilal Vora

Bottom: Awasthi receiving the 'Eminent Chemical Engineer' award of the Indian Institute of Chemical Engineers from the then Vice President of India, Krishan Kant

Top: Awasthi being conferred an Honorary Doctorate Degree by the University of Agricultural Sciences, Dharwad (2006)

Bottom: Receiving the Eminent Cooperator Award from former Prime Minister of India, H.D. Deve Gowda

Top: Awasthi receiving the Dr Davidson Fame Award (2000)

Bottom: Awasthi being conferred a doctoral degree by Vikram University, Ujjain (2008)

Top: With his wife Rekha at the Taj Mahal (1977)

Centre: With his mother Durgavati and sons Amol and Manu

Bottom: Reciting verses of Ramayana to his mother Durgavati

Top: With his late father-in-law, the renowned Hindi writer Shrilal Shukla

Centre: The Awasthi family at the Dal Lake (1986)

Bottom: The Awasthi family with former President of India, Pranab Mukherjee

Top: With his younger sister Rekha

Centre: The Awasthi family with former Prime Minister of India, Atal Bihari Vajpayee (2001)

Bottom: Former Prime Minister of India, Atal Bihari Vajpayee, blessing Awasthi's son Anupam (Manu) and Aarti on their wedding

Top: With his wife Rekha

Bottom: Awasthi over the years

FIVE

MAKING WAVES

The new millennium brought new hope, new opportunities and some new and unexpected challenges—as well as the wrath of God. The logic of economic liberalization had found wide acceptance across the political spectrum. This consensus was being reflected in higher growth rates that were lifting all the boats in the ocean. New sectors were being opened up to private participation. India was on the move!

IFFCO's business was limited to fertilizers, which wasn't a commercially sound strategy. Despite the reforms process, the prices of fertilizers were still controlled by the government. This limited the profit potential of the industry. Awasthi began to look for opportunities in businesses that could help farmers and also bring good returns for the company.

'It isn't wise to keep all your eggs in one basket,' he said.

'The government decided to open up the insurance sector to private investors in 1998. At that time, the Life Insurance Corporation (LIC) was the only life insurance company and there were four general insurance companies. We thought: there is less competition and more opportunities for us to grow in this sector,' said Awasthi.

It would also enable IFFCO to provide protection to farmers from accidents, hardships and untimely deaths.

Thus, the insurance industry ticked both boxes.

IFFCO's network of cooperatives and its reach in rural areas would enable it to do good business on a long-term sustainable basis. Awasthi constituted a committee of in-house executives to draw up a feasibility report on the prospects of the insurance business in India and how IFFCO could create a niche for itself in this sector.

The committee submitted its report in favour of this diversification, and the board gave its in-principle approval for IFFCO to enter the general insurance business on 24 January 2000.

IFFCO conducted another study to look for a credible business partner. A senior team researched all options and, after much deliberation, selected Tokio Marine, then the fifth-largest insurance company in the world, with a presence in forty-one countries, as its partner for the general insurance business.

Then, things moved fast. In September 2000, a JV company named IFFCO-Tokio General Insurance Company was formed; in October 2000, the company got the licence from the Insurance Regulatory and Development Authority (IRDA), and in December 2000, the company started its business.

IFFCO had other options available. As many as thirty-two foreign insurance companies had expressed interest in partnering with it. Among them were several leading American and European companies, but Awasthi's mind was clear—in addition to business logic, the ideological moorings and moral values of the partner should match those of IFFCO's.

Japan is an Asian country, and it has similar cultural and moral values. Like Indians, the Japanese treasure human relations, family values, hospitality and respect and care for elders in society. Then, Japan has a very good cooperative system in agriculture, insurance and other sectors. Its companies have brought about several innovations in crop insurance- and savings-related insurance schemes.

That was why IFFCO chose Tokio Marine as its partner. IFFCO-Tokio

General Insurance (ITGI) was formed with an authorized share capital of ₹125 crore and issued and subscribed capital of ₹100 crore. It was agreed that IFFCO would hold a 74 per cent share in the JV and Tokio Marine would hold the remaining 26 per cent.

The terms of the agreement between the partners stipulated that IFFCO would get to nominate the chairman of the company, while Tokio Marine would select the vice chairman. Both partner companies would jointly choose the managing director. The appointment of Director, Finance, would be within the exclusive purview of IFFCO.

There was a condition that Tokio Marine's shareholding would never exceed IFFCO's in the JV. It was also specified that the number of Tokio Marine directors on the board would never exceed that of IFFCO's.

'It is a matter of pride that the JV agreement we drafted turned out to be a masterpiece. The IRDA uses it in its guidelines for JVs in India,' said R.P. Singh with obvious pride.

The profitability challenge

The next step was to agree on a business plan. The Japanese partner said the company would run in losses for the first five years and then break even. It would start earning profits only after that.

Awasthi had other ideas. He said, 'Our owners are poor farmers. We can't afford a business where the gestation period is so long. We expect profits from the next year.'

'Mr Awasthi, we know the insurance business, and we know, for sure, that we can't earn profits in the first five years. You should not worry about that. After all, we are also investing our money,' the Japanese partner said.

Awasthi replied, 'You may be right that in the insurance business it is usual to earn profits only after five years, but I am used to doing things that are unusual.'

He took it as a challenge. IFFCO was paying around ₹40 crore to ₹50 crore as annual premium to insure its plants. But IRDA has put a limit on that: companies cannot give all their insurance business to associate firms. He used all his influence and relationships to bring the insurance mandates of big organizations to IFFCO-Tokio.

The company reached break even in three years. From then on, it started earning profits. IFFCO-Tokio has been making steady progress since then. It is the fourth-largest private general insurance company in India.

Recruitment magic

When IFFCO-Tokio began recruitments, it faced a challenge. India had a limited talent pool since insurance had been a closed sector till then. Only the public sector had trained and experienced personnel. Everyone was eyeing them; so, their market rates were very high—much higher than the pay scales at IFFCO.

If IFFCO-Tokio were to match those rates, it could potentially create dissonance and resentment in the ranks of the parent organization.

Awasthi had an alternative plan. He said, 'You select a person. Don't negotiate the salary. Let that be done by us. If a person goes to Reliance, Bajaj or Cholamandalam for a hundred thousand rupees, then he will come to IFFCO-Tokio for eighty thousand rupees.'

The Japanese partners were incredulous. They asked, 'Why will they do that?'

'You will understand that in due course of time.'

R.P. Singh recalls Awasthi's honest message to the recruits: 'We are an established organization. We have our own brand value and work ethics. Here, there is a sense of pride in the organization, a very cosy work atmosphere, and absolutely no stress. But the compensation is not that much. The choice is yours.'

Almost 90 per cent of the candidates accepted the IFFCO-Tokio offers.

The IFFCO managing director attributes this to the parent company's brand value and goodwill.

Helping farmers

From the first day, Awasthi was clear in his mind that IFFCO-Tokio had to benefit farmers. It launched a scheme called Sankat Haran Bima Yojana. When a farmer buys a bag of IFFCO fertilizer from a cooperative society, he gets free insurance of ₹4,000 against personal accidents for a year. The receipt for the purchase is his insurance policy; it carries his name, the name of the person nominated by him and his address. The maximum amount of compensation under Sankat Haran is ₹1 lakh. The slogan of the policy is '*Khaad to Khaad, Beema Bhi Saath* [Fertilizers with free insurance].'

The policy is very farmer friendly, and claims are settled without haggling. IFFCO-Tokio does not engage with independent surveyors from the outside to settle these claims. Since IFFCO's associate cooperative societies are the distribution channel for this policy, they assist IFFCO-Tokio in maintaining the necessary records and receipts, which are evidence for payment of compensation. These societies also assist farmers in completing the paperwork for claims and coordinates with IFFCO-Tokio till the claim amount is disbursed.

This scheme was launched in September 2001. Since then, over two crore farmers have benefited from it. IIFFCO pays Re 1 as premium on each bag of fertilizer. IFFCO-Tokio generates more revenues than it disburses in compensation during a year and so the scheme is profitable.

'Tokio Marine executives initially opposed the idea, but when I explained to them that this was necessary to popularize insurance in rural India, they understood and agreed. Today, this insurance scheme is known all over the world. The United Nations (UN) has also praised the Sankat Haran Bima Yojana,' said Awasthi.

Similarly, IFFCO-Mitsubishi Corporation (MC) launched a scheme called Kisan Suraksha Bima Yojana. If a farmer buys an IFFCO product of more than ₹150, then he automatically gets insurance for an amount that is 6.67 times his purchase. So, if a farmer buys IFFCO pesticides for ₹10,000, he automatically gets an insurance of ₹66,700. To make it affordable and easy for farmers, their purchases of IFFCO products over a year are aggregated for the purpose of calculating the sum insured.

The company also launched several other schemes to benefit small farmers and their families. Under the Mahila Suraksha Bima Yojana, for example, women are provided with an insurance cover of ₹50,000 against personal accidents at an annual premium of only ₹20. The scheme was launched in 2005 on International Women's Day.

'Our biggest achievement is that we have taken insurance to rural India,' said Awasthi, 'and this has provided relief to the farmers in the country.'

A wise investment

The total valuation of IFFCO-Tokio as of 2022 is more than ₹20,000 crore. In 2016, IFFCO divested 21.64 per cent of its shareholding in the company in favour of Tokio Marine at ₹2,380.4 crore. IPL, which had 1.36 per cent in the company, sold out to Tokio Marine for ₹149.6 crore. At present, IFFCO holds 51 per cent while Tokio Marine holds 49 per cent in the company.

Gujarat earthquake: IFFCO to the rescue

On the morning of 26 January 2001, while the country was celebrating Republic Day, a severe earthquake struck Gujarat at 9.00 a.m. Nearly 20,000 people died and over 6,00,000 were left homeless. The epicentre was at Anjar, 20–30 kilometres from IFFCO's Kandla plant.

Awasthi reached Ahmedabad the same day on an evening flight and drove to Kalol, 300 kilometres away. Fortunately, the earthquake hadn't caused much damage to the plant. A portion of its boundary wall had caved in and some minor cracks had developed in the buildings of the township.

But later, when he wanted to visit Kandla, Awasthi found the drivers were hesitant.

Tremors were still being felt in the region. Finally, a driver (Pandey-ji) agreed to drive him to Kandla, which was about three hundred kilometres away. They set out at 10.30 p.m. There was complete silence all along the way. There was neither any light, nor any human being to be seen.

'We reached Kandla around four in the morning. Everything seemed to be at a standstill. It looked like a ghost town,' said Awasthi.

S.K. Mishra, IFFCO's unit head, was shaking when Awasthi arrived. Awasthi had to take charge of the situation and he did.

The Indian Oil Corporation (IOC) township in front of IFFCO's township had taken a hit. 'Our township had not collapsed, but the guest house had suffered extensive damage. It was not possible to stay there, but I thought I should take a shower because the bathroom seemed fine,' said Awasthi.

He called all the drivers and asked them to collect all the diesel that was there. He sent a person to IOC for a tanker of diesel.

The tanker arrived. All the cranes and buses were tanked up. Simultaneously, Awasthi ordered his team to start preparing khichdi. Awasthi's sense of purpose inspired his executives.

They took out all the cranes and buses and started rescuing the people still trapped in the debris. A three-storey school building in Anjar had caved in. There were children trapped inside. IFFCO's crane drivers pulled out several children. The government agencies came after a few hours. Until then, the IFFCO team had been the only source of hope for the victims.

'We made lots of khichdi. People came in hordes to eat. The phone network had collapsed. When the satellite phones started, Awasthi ordered his team at Kalol to send supplies. Next day, a truckload of blankets, tarpaulins, rice, pulses, vegetables and other items arrived. Our people went to remote villages in the interiors of Kutch where rescue teams usually do not go. Many lives were saved. I lived in a tent for a week,' recalls Awasthi.

At the head office, he set up a control room and directed an executive director to coordinate relief operations and maintain communication with government agencies. Awasthi proposed to the board of directors that IFFCO should set up a separate fund to rehabilitate the victims of natural calamities such as floods, earthquakes, and cyclones.

The board appreciated the idea and the Kisan Sewa Fund was founded with capital of ₹10 crore. The officers and employees of IFFCO contributed an additional ₹1 crore. Kisan Sewa did very good work in Gujarat.

'We adopted seven villages in Kutch for resettlement and built more than 600 houses there. Atal Bihari Vajpayee was the Prime Minister of India at that time. We went to meet him and donated ₹50 lakh to the Prime Minister's Relief Fund. Later, we converted the Kisan Sewa Fund to the IFFCO Kisan Sewa Trust (IKST) [on 9 February 2001] to help victims of natural calamities. It also provides help for the medical treatment of poor people in villages,' said Awasthi.

A safety net for distressed farmers

Rajkumar Tripathi*, a nominated director on the board of IFFCO, said about Awasthi, 'The cooperative movement in Uttar Pradesh had nearly died. Udai Shanker Awasthi is the man who infused new life into the cooperative societies because of his concern for farmers.'

'That farmer could be anyone. The only condition is that he should

*He died in 2019.

be recommended by an IFFCO member from that area. Then, there are scholarships for the children of poor farmers. If the child is a good student and maintains a first division, then scholarships are given for his/her higher education,' said Tripathi.

He recounted the tale of a daily wager whose son topped the Uttar Pradesh board examinations. The result was announced in the evening. Early next morning, the IFFCO area manager was there at his doorstep with a ₹2 lakh cheque.

'There are numerous such examples,' he adds.

'We support farmers with whatever we can. We give them medical and educational support via IKST. In case of calamities, we rush to the people with relief materials. We have a 360-degree relationship them. It's not only about giving them fertilizers,' said Awasthi.

Twist in the tale

The year 2001 held another nasty surprise for Awasthi. The term of the existing board of directors had expired, and the new board was to be constituted that year. Om Prakash Chautala was the Chief Minister of Haryana. He wanted his son, Ajay Chautala, to be the next chairman of IFFCO.

This was a disturbing development. IFFCO had a tradition of not electing active politicians as the chairman. Several chairmen had ventured into active politics later, but they were not in active politics during their tenure at IFFCO.

'We have had representation from all political parties on our board, but IFFCO has always been a politically neutral organization. So, it was very important for us that this great tradition continued,' said Awasthi.

The National Democratic Alliance (NDA) government was in power at the Centre. Om Prakash Chautala's party was an important constituent of the NDA. Sukhdev Singh Dhindsa, Union Minister of Chemicals and

Fertilizers, invited the directors of IFFCO to dinner one day. Most of the IFFCO directors refused to attend. Awasthi was present with two or three directors. Om Prakash Chautala told him, '*Arre, sahkarita mein to sab kuchh consensus se hota hai; kal Ajay ko chairman bana dena* [Everything in cooperatives happens by consensus; so make Ajay the chairman tomorrow].'

'The campaign to install Ajay Chautala as the chairman of IFFCO was the brainchild of Satbir Singh Kadiyan, who had been a chairman of IFFCO in the past,' said R.P. Singh.

Kadiyan had joined Chautala's party, the Indian National Lok Dal, and was the Speaker of the Haryana Assembly at that time. When the news broke that Ajay Chautala wanted to become the chairman of IFFCO, everyone in IFFCO was worried because Om Prakash Chautala did not have a good image.

But there was no strong candidate in IFFCO to fight Ajay Chautala. Surinder Jakhar had been chairman twice. There is a rule in IFFCO that no one can become chairman more than twice. No one else was ready to stand against Chautala. There was a pall of fear around the election.

A cooperative member from Bihar, Ajit Singh, agreed to fight against Ajay Chautala. The annual general meeting (AGM) was organized at the Talkatora Stadium. There were apprehensions that antisocial elements from Haryana might try to use force to swing the election in Ajay Chautala's favour. But the Delhi Police made tight security arrangements and did not allow any unauthorized people to enter the venue.

Ajay Chautala, director of the Haryana State Marketing Federation, came to IFFCO's AGM as a delegate. He easily defeated Mangi Lal Danga and won the director's election. Busloads of people from Haryana arrived, shouting slogans for him. A truckload of garlands and flowers also arrived. His supporters were sure of his victory.

Awasthi stood up and said, 'In the history of IFFCO so far, all the chairmen have been unanimously elected. The election means that there is lack of trust among the board members. There have been differences of opinion among the board members, but the final decision has always been unanimous. Therefore, I request the board of directors that the chairman and the vice chairman be elected unanimously.'

Some directors also put forth their views. Jakhar said Srinivas Gowda should be the chairman as he had been the chairman of KRIBHCO and had the experience to lead IFFCO. 'Let Ajay Chautala be the vice chairman this time. He can become the chairman next time,' he said.

But Ajay Chautala did not agree. He would be the chairman or nothing.

It was finally decided that a vote would take place. A few moments later, Ajay Chautala got up and said, 'I withdraw.'

He may have sensed that he would lose.

Srinivas Gowda was then unanimously elected the chairman and N.P. Patel was the vice chairman.

Trouble in Senegal

'I joined IFFCO in 2003 and ICS was one of the first projects I was confronted with,' said Manish Gupta. 'It was facing financial problems and was not generating enough revenues to meet its financial obligations.'

ICS was set up in Senegal in 1977 to produce phosphoric acid, which is needed as a raw material for fertilizer production in India. This was in line with Awasthi's philosophy of promoting India's food security by securing IFFCO's raw material supplies from across the globe. India lacks the raw materials to make sufficient quantities of phosphoric acid.

The company was under the control of the Government of Senegal, which held 46 per cent of its shares. IFFCO was the other major shareholder, with 26 per cent. Some West African countries such as Cameroon, Niger and a few others held 2–3 per cent shares each. The Government of India and SPIC also had small stakes in it.

There was a change of regime in Senegal when the project started.

The new president called Awasthi for a meeting and demanded some favours. Awasthi was taken aback. He hadn't expected a head of state to speak like that. He politely refused to succumb to the unfair demands made by the president. Then he got up and left the room.

'I don't know if he made a mistake, or if I made a mistake. Perhaps I should have handled the situation more diplomatically. He was so upset that he made it his personal agenda to close ICS, and I was hell-bent on not allowing the company to die.'

Next, he was asked to change the Managing Director, Mr Cama, who was close to Mr Diouf, the earlier president.

Awasthi said, 'No, I will not.'

This tug-of-war continued for six months.

One day, he was called by a minister, Mr Savane. He met Awasthi with courtesy, offered coffee and snacks and then got to the point, 'Mr Awasthi, we will arrest Mr Cama if he does not resign today. You go and tell him to resign.' He added, 'There is a person waiting outside. He is Mr Gomes. He will be the new managing director.'

Now this was quite a situation! The proverbial irresistible force had met an immovable object. Something had to give. By this time, Awasthi had realized that it was a custom in African countries for appointing new chief executives whenever a new regime was ushered in.

He went to meet Mr Cama and told him what had happened. Mr Cama understood the situation and said, 'I will resign.'

The bankers, who had lent money to ICS, then said, 'If Mr Cama is going as CMD, then we want this post to be split.' The loan agreement stipulated that Mr Cama would continue as CMD till the project was completed. They added, 'We will not accept the new man as both. Mr Awasthi should be the chairman. Mr Gomes can be the managing director.'

Awasthi was reluctant to take up the responsibility that was being thrust upon him, but the bankers were insistent. He told Mr Savane about the new development.

'We don't mind this arrangement, but Mr Cama has to go.'

Awasthi was appointed chairman of ICS in 2000.

When ICS was conceived, the idea was to convert part of the production of phosphoric acid into finished fertilizers in Senegal for its local economy. ICS had a plant to manufacture complex fertilizers. But 85 per cent of its production was to be shipped to IFFCO. Though IFFCO was a minority partner in this venture, everyone respected Awasthi and looked up to him for advice and guidance. So, the Indian partner had an influence in ICS out of proportion to its shareholding.

IFFCO decided to expand ICS at the same time as Kandla was being expanded. Before that, it made an important suggestion. 'The mine that supplied rock phosphate to our phosphoric acid plant was a separate company. We suggested to the Senegalese government that these two companies should be merged. They liked our idea, and the two companies were merged. After that, we expanded the plant,' said Awasthi.

But the plant kept having problems, so the primary production of phosphoric acid went to IFFCO. Production had started to suffer. There wasn't enough money to invest in repairs and maintenance of the plant.

'The market conditions were bad. Around this time, the Senegalese government forced a change in the management of ICS, which, coupled with some other factors, turned the company sick,' said Gupta. When a company's net worth is eroded by 50 per cent, it legally becomes sick. That's what happened to ICS.

The plant somehow managed to keep producing phosphoric acid, but at lower capacities. Its output kept reducing every year because of plant breakdowns. ICS seemed to be slowly and inexorably heading towards certain bankruptcy.

'I did not allow the company to die,' Awasthi asserts with undiminished passion. 'There were very poor people employed there; they would suffer. And India needed phosphoric acid and IFFCO needed assured raw material supplies. If ICS had died, phosphoric acid prices would have shot sky-high. So, I put in all my effort and ensured that the company survived. And I succeeded!'

Mr Bourgi, a lawyer representing ICS, adds, 'As soon as Mr Awasthi realized that the company was on the verge of bankruptcy, he invested himself day and night, travelled a lot to Senegal, met the managers, the workers and the politicians. A lot of money was needed...fresh agreements had to be made with creditors. But thanks to his personality and his personal investment, the creditors continued to trust ICS.'

Against all odds, Awasthi kept the company running for close to fifteen years. Banks were asked to restructure their loans, and still more money was needed. Awasthi used his persuasive powers and brought in the Archean Group from Chennai to invest in the company in 2008. IFFCO remained an active partner. The Archean Group relied a lot on IFFCO because it had been a partner in ICS for a long time. Awasthi continued to lead the company as chairman, and it started doing well.

But, after a few years, there was a major accident from which it could never recover.

ICS's financials became weak again, and it once again faced the prospect of bankruptcy. The company started defaulting on its debt payments. Another phase of restructuring began and culminated with the induction of the Indo Rama Group as an investor in ICS in 2016. Awasthi resigned as chairman when Indo Rama came in.

There are now three major shareholders in ICS—Indo Rama, IFFCO (7 per cent) and the Government of Senegal (15 per cent). The Government of India also owns half a per cent, which IFFCO had given to the body from its own share. The company is doing well once again.

'Under a new agreement with ICS, 85 per cent of its acid production comes to IFFCO. We have also put up a phosphoric acid plant in Jordan. So, there is no shortage of phosphoric acid in IFFCO,' said Gupta.

Awasthi played a pivotal role in all these transactions but also gave his team the authority to take decisions within a given set of parameters.

'Whenever the opportunity came, I did what I thought was right for my country. I invested in Senegal, then the plants in Oman and Jordan, then I started a company in Dubai. All these new ventures were conceived and set up with the larger objective of making India self-reliant in fertilizers,' he said.

On the wings of autonomy

Following the enactment of the Multi-State Cooperative Societies (MSCS) Act, 2002 by the Vajpayee-led NDA government, IFFCO attained full cooperative ownership and became autonomous in July 2004.

Until then, it had been governed first by the Multi-Unit Cooperative Societies Act, 1942, and then by the Multi-State Cooperative Societies Act, 1984. These acts created a government-dominated framework that did not accommodate the long-standing demand of cooperatives for more freedom to work and take decisions. Though the 2002 Act granted cooperatives like IFFCO full autonomy, a practical problem arose. The government held a significant percentage of shares. How could they be redeemed and at what value?

The MSCS Act, 2002 clearly stated that redemption of the government's equity stake would take place at par value. This means if a share had a par value of ₹10, the government would get only that much. If there are 1 lakh shares of ₹10 each, then the total value of the equity would be ₹10 lakh.

The other new provision was that redemption would take place either with the consent of the government or in accordance with the provisions of the by-laws of the cooperative societies, which are like the Articles of Association of the Companies Act.

Now, every cooperative has its own by-laws which are mandatorily subservient to the provisions of the MSCS Act, 2002. After the promulgation of the Act, it was made mandatory that every cooperative society amend its by-laws to make them consistent with the new Act. Wherever they were inconsistent, they were deemed inoperative and void and, in their place, the MSCS Act, 2002 was to be applied.

The procedure for the amendment of by-laws is that the general body of the cooperative society first amends them by a two-thirds majority, and then the amended by-laws are sent to the Central Registrar of Cooperative Societies for registration.

'In our case also, we devised a formula that every quarter we would retire government equity to the extent that they were subscribed by existing and new member societies. That formula was adopted and the amended by-laws were sent to the Central Registrar of Cooperative Societies for registration,' said R.P. Singh.

The registrar wrote a letter to the Department of Fertilizers for its comments but did not receive any response. Following this, it registered the amended by-laws.

The other very important provision of the MSCS Act, 2002 was that it created a distinction between cooperative societies on the basis of the percentage of government equity held by them. If the government equity was more than 51 per cent, a special audit by the government was permitted; supersession of the board could be done by the government and the managing director would be appointed by the government.

IFFCO had five government directors on its board. But the MSCS Act, 2002 clearly stated that there would be three such directors if government equity was more than 51 per cent, two if its share were between 26 per cent and 51 per cent, and one if it held less than 26 per cent.

It was also very clearly stated that there would be no special audit of cooperative societies where the government's share was less than 51 per cent.

'It became more or less like the Companies Act, 1956, where the government doesn't interfere in the affairs of companies it does not own,' said R.P. Singh.

There was one more provision—which was present in the earlier Act too—that if a cooperative society has a large membership, then it can face problems in managing its general body meetings. The Act has a provision for a smaller general body to be constituted where the numbers are restricted to a maximum of 1,000, and also that that general body would be called the representative general body (RGB).

IFFCO has an RGB of 1,000 members who come from various constituencies spread all over the country. The new Act also clearly stipulated that the number of directors, excluding the functional and co-opted directors, should not exceed twenty-one.

Ten directorships were allotted to the eighteen State Cooperative Marketing Federations. They elected ten directors from among themselves. Three were government nominees. The remaining eight directors came from the 36,000-member cooperative societies spread across the country.

As IFFCO started retiring government equity, the number of government directors started falling, and the number of directors elected by the 36,000 societies started increasing—from eight to nine, then ten and, eventually, eleven.

IFFCO had become an autonomous multi-state cooperative society, wholly owned by the cooperatives of the country. It had finally realized its long-cherished goal!

Repatriation of the government equity began in January 2003 and was completed by July 2004. In one and a half years, the entire government equity (of ₹289 crore) was repatriated by cooperative societies of the country.

But this did not go down well with some senior officials of the Department of Fertilizers. They said there ought to have been an agreement between the Department of Fertilizers and IFFCO before the repatriation had begun. Some senior officers of the Ministry of Finance also joined them in their protest. They said the repatriation at par value was not justified.

But the Department of Agriculture and Cooperation rejected their objections on the grounds that one does not invest in cooperative societies to seek profits like one would invest in private companies on the stock exchange. Also, both autonomy and valuation flowed from an Act of Parliament. These provisions could be changed only by another Act of Parliament, it said.

'This pronouncement from the Department of Agriculture and Cooperation settled the issue in our favour and they [Department of Fertilizers] started accepting our cheques,' said Awasthi.

But before the repatriation could be completed, the 14th Lok Sabha elections (2004) were held, and a fresh government came to power at the Centre. The fresh Minister of Chemicals and Fertilizers started a fresh controversy over this issue. They said that such a huge disinvestment without a proper valuation exercise was a huge scam. They first wrote to the Department of Agriculture and Cooperation, which reiterated its earlier stand that there was nothing wrong with the repatriation and that it was taking place as per the provisions of the MSCS Act, 2002. Then they wrote to the Ministry of Law and Justice, the Cabinet Secretariat and the Department of Expenditure.

Awasthi found himself engaged in another tug-of-war—this time, with a minister in the Government of India. The usual trick in such cases is that the government begins to tighten any screws it can find till its opponent buckles under the pressure. But despite the pressure, Awasthi did not budge an inch.

The whole issue was examined once again. Finally, the law ministry gave its opinion that the repatriation was irreversible. The Attorney General said that once the money was taken, it was presumed that the government had given consent. This is how the issue was settled at that time.

A fresh controversy started once again when KRIBHCO started repatriating the government's shares. The Department of Fertilizers issued a directive to KRIBHCO to stop repatriation and amend its by-laws to restore *status quo ante*. There is a section in the MSCS Act, 2002, which empowers the government to issue directives to a cooperative society if it holds 51 per cent or more equity in it.

KRIBHCO moved the Delhi High Court against the directive, citing IFFCO's precedent and the opinion of the Attorney General. The high court ruled in favour of KRIBHCO in 2008. The government did not move the Supreme Court, so the matter ended there.

Again, in 2010–2011, a politician took it upon himself to 'expose' Awasthi and IFFCO. He fabricated serious charges against both IFFCO and Awasthi and sent them to the president, the prime minister, the finance minister, and all the concerned departments. The whole issue was re-examined.

But since the high court had already ruled in favour of KRIBHCO and no appeal had been filed by the government in the Supreme Court, the issue was closed once again.

'Whenever a new government comes, this issue is raised—only the manner changes. In 2014, a fresh government came to power at the Centre and, in 2016, the issue was raised yet again. A fresh secretary came to the Department of Fertilizers. He must have had some serious problems with IFFCO because as soon as he arrived, he started raking up all the past issues,' said Awasthi.

The secretary wrote to the Central Registrar of Cooperative Societies that the registration of the by-laws of IFFCO was wrong. He argued that before the MSCS Act, 2002 there was a provision in IFFCO's by-laws that no by-law could be amended without the permission of the government, as long as the government had a stake in it. Since this amendment was put together without the permission of the government, the registration should be cancelled and *status quo ante* restored, he argued. The registrar said it was beyond its authority to do so. Then the secretary wrote letters to the Ministry of Law, the Directorate of Enforcement, the Central Bureau of Investigation and the Comptroller and Auditor General.

He also made an appeal after a lapse of over 14 years before the appellate authority under the Multi-State Cooperative Societies Act in the year 2017.

As of now, the matter is once again before the court. IFFCO has received interim relief from the Delhi High Court where the case is pending.

Separation of IFFCO and KRIBHCO

There is a provision in the MSCS Act, 2002 that no cooperative society can hold shares in any other cooperative society with which it competes for business. Since IFFCO and KRIBHCO are in the same business and held shares in each other, the Department of Fertilizers issued a directive to KRIBHCO to amend its by-laws to remove IFFCO nominees from its board of directors and repatriate IFFCO's share.

KRIBHCO amended its by-laws and returned ₹97 crore to IFFCO. IFFCO also returned KRIBHCO's investment—a meagre amount of ₹5 lakh. The separation took place in the last quarter of 2004.

Autonomy opened up new opportunities

'Autonomy opened up new vistas for expansion. We visualized something bigger, producing everything that a farmer requires under cooperative ownership,' said Awasthi.

The situation was dire. Farmers did not have any insurance. There was no agrochemical for their crops. They lacked quality seeds. There was no talk of how to make their land green and increase forest cover. They did not have information about modern technology. There was no place where they could be trained and empowered to adopt new technologies.

'We also realized that farmers are completely ignorant about their health problems. They do not know when their blood pressure is high, when their sugar level goes up, when their eyesight becomes weak...not until these become serious problems,' Singh adds.

Pramod Kumar Singh* was a director of IFFCO from Uttarakhand. 'He saved my life,' Singh said about Awasthi, IFFCO's managing director.

Singh had had a kidney transplant. IFFCO ensured his treatment till the last day. This is not an isolated case. Everyone in the IFFCO family is insured for treatment without any budgetary limit.

'Saving life is the priority—not the cost of treatment,' Awasthi said.

This has helped create strong personal bonds between Awasthi, IFFCO, its members and other stakeholders.

A large-hearted ambassador of India

Luc Maene, the long-time director general of IFA, remembers the time he had gone to Cape Town in 2006 for an IFA conference.

'There was a cultural programme in the evening in honour of the IFA delegates. The who's who of the world fertilizer industry was present there. There were executives who earned a hundred times more money than Awasthi. Some chief executive officers (CEOs) of American companies earn bonuses of hundreds of crores a year,' he said.

The programme included a dance performance by disadvantaged children. When the dance ended, Awasthi raised his hand. He said, 'My name is U.S. Awasthi. I represent India. In India, I represent the Indian Farmers and Fertilizers Cooperative [IFFCO]. I'm donating $10,000 for these children.'

'Everyone was stunned for a while and then the clapping started, and soon reached a crescendo. It was a wonderful moment,' said Maene.

---

*He died in 2021.

A new home for IFFCO

It is 9.00 a.m. The IFFCO head office is alert about the arrival of its managing director. A white Ambassador drives into the portico. The security chief rushes towards the car. Awasthi steps out, buttoning his blazer. The officer walks him to the lift.

Awasthi sits on the fourth floor, the top floor where the joint managing director, marketing director and Director, Technical also sit.

The staff of the Managing Director's Secretariat have already arrived. In his impressive chamber, lined with paintings by modern masters and amateurs, Awasthi settles down to work with a cup of tea—after a brief puja.

The location of the office building is also very impressive. It is built on a 3,020 square metre plot in the Saket District Centre in south Delhi. It is just behind Select City Walk and adjacent to DLF Mall. There are many other malls, restaurants and swanky office buildings in the neighbourhood. There is also a five-star hotel within walking distance.

'These malls were not there when we bought the plot in 2004,' reveals an IFFCO insider. 'Select City Walk came up a year after we moved here in 2006. The area flourished after that.'

The foundation stone-laying ceremony and the inauguration of IFFCO House were both memorable events that bore Awasthi's signature.

'We got soil from all over India, and we got water from all the rivers in the country. Our people came from all over India. We mixed the soil and the water and made the brick. Then the puja was done. Everybody touched the brick before it was laid. Similarly, when the office was inaugurated, everybody touched the scissors before it was handed over to the chairman for him to cut the ribbon,' said Awasthi.

IFFCO stakeholders from all over the country were present at the inauguration. Surinder Jakhar was the chairman of IFFCO at the time. He said, 'This is the seat of power where famers are the kings. It is their property and their wealth. We are the custodians.'

A rich collection of art

There is a painting of a wheat field behind Awasthi's table. This is done with oil on canvas by Paramjit Singh. Awasthi had bought it in 1998, after completing the expansion of the plants and had called it 'Golden Land'.

On the same wall, in the right corner, there is a painting by Satish Gujral. This is done in acrylic on canvas. He bought this painting in 2008 after reviving the Paradeep plant, and called it 'Riding High on Achievements'.

An interviewer had once asked Awasthi if he had silently celebrated his triumphs by acquiring these paintings. A big smile had spread over his face, but he did not respond.

Sunil Savane is in charge of the paintings. He said, 'He [Awasthi] has a very rich knowledge of paintings. We have a collection of around 350 paintings. He knows about all of them. We also have paintings and sculptures presented by our JV partners and technology suppliers like OMIFCO, Jordan India Fertiliser Company and Haldor Topsoe. There are also gifts from the Cooperative League of USA (CLUSA), Agricultural Cooperative Development International/Volunteers in Overseas Cooperative Assistance (ACDI/VOCA) and IFA.'

Awasthi said, 'There are around thirty-five paintings by very famous artists like M.F. Husain, F.N. Souza, Ram Kumar, S.H. Raza, Satish Gujral, Anjolie Ela Menon, Akbar Padamsee, Jatin Das, Shanti Dave, Krishen Khanna, Laxman Pai, G.R. Santosh, B.C. Sanyal, Redappa Naidu and many others.'

'Then there are middle-grade painters,' he adds. 'We have some paintings by painters who were students when these were bought. Now they are famous artists.'

'We also buy paintings of amateur artists. In the golden jubilee year, we organized a workshop of twenty-five artists in J.J. School of Art, Mumbai. We supplied them with the materials and gave them awards. Every year, our annual report carries a painting from our collection on its cover. We have also published two beautiful coffee table books on our art treasures,' he said.

These art treasures are distributed across the IFFCO building. There are freshly garlanded statues of Lord Ganesha and some female deities as one enters the premises. A painting of a dancing deity adorns the wall behind the reception.

Almost all the cabins in the building have displayed similar paintings. An interior designer who worked on the IFFCO office said the entire design was guided by how the paintings would be displayed. These paintings and artworks give the IFFCO head office a very distinctive air.

Previously, IFFCO instituted the 'Jawaharlal Nehru Memorial IFFCO Lecture' in 1982 to promote a holistic development of Indian cultural ethos. The lecture has since been delivered by Dr Desmond M. Tutu, Dr M.S. Swaminathan, Dr P.J. Kurien, Dr Karan Singh, Dr A.P.J. Abdul Kalam, Dr Girish Karnad and other eminent personalities from different fields.

Taking technology to India's farmers

In 2007, IFFCO collaborated with Bharti Airtel, then India's largest mobile telephone operator, and Star Global Resources to launch IFFCO Kisan Sanchar. This collaboration provides farmers with mobile advisory services, has the IFFCO Kisan Agriculture app, and also provides access to the IFFCO Kisan Call Centre. In addition to these services, it sells items like cattle feed and honey. IFFCO Kisan Sanchar also helps farmers upgrade the quality of their products and provides an avenue for them to sell their produce directly to manufacturing units.

'There is television, there are telephones, there are many other means of communication, but the farmer is still hungry for information. He doesn't get what he wants. And often, because of that, he is unable to take the right decision, which can help him. That was why we floated this rural telephony company,' said Awasthi.

To avail the services under this scheme, a farmer has to buy a green sim for ₹45. It entitles him to five free messages every day all his life. If he maintains the talktime, he is connected to a twenty-four-hour helpline. The company is making good progress. IFFCO Kisan Sanchar has developed apps on which farmers can buy and sell their produce. Now, it has started giving loans as well.

'Our objective now is to transform IFFCO Kisan Sanchar into an instrument of change,' said Sandeep Malhotra, CEO, IFFCO Kisan Sanchar. 'When it was launched, the idea was far ahead of its time. Nobody anticipated the penetration of mobile phones. Now we need to go deeper... to engage the farmers in a meaningful way, which we are doing with the mobile advisory services helpline.'

IFFCO Kisan Sanchar achieves this with its agronomists, who are present in every state, and who travel to the fields, organize farmers into the groups, look at their problems from a crop growing perspective and help them adopt the best practices in agriculture, as well as prescribe better pre-harvesting and post-harvesting techniques.

'Once that is done then you can also handhold the farmers and help them realize better prices for their produce,' Malhotra added.

'Then, education is very important. People will pay for education. Anything given free does not carry any value. If the farmer pays even ₹10, he thinks he is paying, so he is getting some value out of it,' he said.

As the telecom sector faced intense competition due to new entrants, it was desirable to start a new line of business in IFFCO Kisan Sanchar. After some deliberation, and following a pilot project, a wholly owned subsidiary, IFFCO Kisan Finance, was formed. It applied for a non-banking financial company (NBFC) licence, which was granted in June 2018. The company commenced its lending business the same month.

Ultimately, besides IFFCO and Star Global, more investors joined as investors. Later, ICICI Bank and South Korea's cooperative venture NH Financial Group's NBFC arm also invested in this company, apart from

Aurum Vriddhi Finance. The company has disbursed secured loans to farmers with an average ticket size of ₹3.6 lakh and has established a reputation for conducting its affairs in an ethical and transparent manner.

Thus, IFFCO Kisan Finance introduced farmers to formal banking channels that give them finance at lower rates than the local moneylenders. This completed the cycle of handholding—from selecting the right seeds, pesticides and fertilizers to helping farmers in their post-harvesting phase; it also provides them with finances, so they are able to sell at a better price.

Kisan SEZ

IFFCO had acquired 2,700 acres of land in Nellore for an ammonia–urea complex. When that project was eventually shelved, IFFCO thought of developing an agro-processing zone there.

'I picked up the model from China. Agriculture in China is very advanced. Farmers there blend organic and green manures with chemical fertilizers. It is mandatory for farmers to keep livestock. Animal waste is recycled into organic fertilizer. They have developed a 30,000 acre agro-processing zone, which is fossil-fuel-free. I have tried to replicate the same model at the Kisan special economic zone (SEZ),' said Awasthi.

Rakesh Kapur, Joint Managing Director, IFFCO, has been leading this project. 'We had land and the area was quite rich in various citrus fruits and other horticultural produce like vegetables. Then, Nellore is close to both Chennai and Bengaluru, so we thought there was significant potential for value addition to local horticultural produce,' said Kapur.

Awasthi went and met the Chief Minister of Andhra Pradesh. 'He explained to the government that we planned to develop the entire area into an agropark,' said Kapur.

An agropark is a cluster of agro-processing industries that share common infrastructure. IFFCO got a consultancy from the Netherlands, which had done lots of work in other countries on developing such agroparks. The foreign consultant felt that European investors would be interested in coming to India to set up agro-processing units.

The government gave the permission for the SEZ. Two to three investors' groups from Europe visited the site and were keen to invest. Then, in 2008, the economic downturn happened, and all investments stopped. These investors did not return.

'We observed that many investors were looking at India as a big market. A European food company said there is ample demand in the country itself, why did it need to export? We realized that an SEZ for agro-processing may not work,' Kapur informed.

So, IFFCO has converted a part of the land into a domestic tariff zone. IFFCO SEZ is the developer of the industrial zone. It has created the infrastructure—water, power, inside roads, drainage, etc. One of its boundary walls is next to a railway line on the busy Calcutta–Chennai route.

'The place has wonderful connectivity. It's on National Highway 5—the Chennai–Calcutta highway,' said Kapur. 'You can load a wagon and it can go up to Chennai port, which is about 45 kilometres away. We are having discussions with some parties for a railway siding there,' said Kapur.

Some large units have set up plants there. Spanish wind turbine maker Gamesa and some of its ancillary units are there. Coke is setting up bottling and fruit juice plants. IFFCO is putting up a large warehouse and biofertilizer plant there too. ArcelorMittal is also considering setting up a steel plant there.

The Kisan SEZ is a very ambitious project undertaken by Awasthi and he is confident it will yield good returns in the future.

Awasthi addresses the UN

The UN Commission on Sustainable Development was established in 1992. As it also dealt with agriculture, IFA had constituted an Agri-Food

Network of farmers, cooperatives, plant protection chemical industries and some agriculture NGOs. It felt the need for strategic partners in order to make itself heard.

Luc Maene managed to get the Agri-Food Network accepted by the UN as a partner entity. So, for the April 1998 conference, they asked IFA to send a panel of names from which it would select one to make an intervention in the conference. For the first time in the history of the UN, somebody not from government would be allowed to speak.

'This was a historic occasion, and everyone wanted that slot—bigwigs from the plant protection chemical industry, farmer groups, cooperatives, everyone was scrambling to get that slot. I did not say anything. I just forwarded Awasthi's name. And as the process developed, Awasthi's name stayed on course,' said Maene.

Awasthi emerged as the favourite to speak because he was from the cooperative sector. Then, from an agricultural perspective, India is a major country. Ultimately, there were two candidates left, one from South America, and Awasthi. The chairman of the Commission of Sustainable Development that year was the Environment Minister of Columbia. He gave the slot to Awasthi.

His speech was postponed twice. Maene went up to the chairman and said, 'Mr Awasthi is getting restless because he was supposed to speak.'

The chairman said, 'We've got a problem. Since he is not a government official, he cannot speak until all the government representatives and all the UN agencies have spoken.'

'Okay. If you do not allow him to speak now, he is going home.'

They let him speak.

Awasthi's intervention was just perfect—very balanced and very composed. It was widely appreciated by everyone.

A movement to save India's soil

The 'Save the Soil' project was Awasthi's response to the crisis in Indian agriculture. IFFCO launched the 'Save the Soil' campaign when it realized that farmers had abandoned their traditional ways of agriculture and had become completely dependent on chemical fertilizers.

'We found soil that used to be fertile, that used to yield good crops, but was increasingly losing its fertility. As a result, the cost of cultivation was increasing. Farmers were having to apply more chemical fertilizers. The quality of crops was suffering, and their yields were declining with every passing year. There are deficiencies of micronutrients in the food cycle,' said Awasthi.

He was clear in his mind: the purpose of chemical fertilizers was not that only chemical fertilizers would be used. The idea was to replenish the deficiency of soil nutrients. 'It did not mean we should abandon organic manures, discard compost and green manuring and stop following crop cycles, which naturally replenish soil deficiencies,' he explains.

A budget of ₹100 crore was allocated and the project was started in 2009 in every district of the country. IFFCO's field officers were given targets. First, they had to collect soil samples from the 500 adopted villages and adjoining areas for tests. They would have to share the reports with the farmers who would then start applying fertilizers in balanced doses, based on the report.

Secondly, farmers had forgotten green and organic manures. The field officers were given the target of growing green manure in the adopted villages, over 20 hectares of land. The seeds of *dhaincha* (green manure) were sent to all the adopted villages.

For organic manure, phospho-sulpho-nitro compost pits were prepared on the land of the farmers. Some chemical fertilizers are also added to the pits. There are eight layers, put one over another in prescribed measures; then, water is poured into the pits and they are covered. In three months, each pit yields four quintals of high-quality compost that is better than most organic manures.

The 'Save the Soil' project also has a biofertilizer component to rejuvenate the soil and increase soil fertility by 15–20 per cent. IFFCO has a biofertilizer unit at its Phulpur plant. Its capacity was increased. New units were established at all its plant locations. Today the company produces about 14 lakh litres of biofertilizers.

Then comes the change in crop cycle. IFFCO launched several large-scale projects to demonstrate the change in crop cycle, incorporating all the components of the 'Save the Soil' project. It christened it 'Soil Rejuvenation and Productivity Enhancement Project', This project gave farmers very good prices. They saw the correct farming technique and the growth in their incomes for themselves.

In the late 1990s, water soluble fertilizers came into the Indian market. The prices varied from ₹170 to ₹220 per kg. Both public and private sector companies began manufacturing them. Water soluble fertilizers are a very useful input. They facilitate better absorption of nutrients from the soil.

Awasthi responded to this new development by importing them and brought the price down to ₹70 per packet. Every other company had to bring their rates down. The net gainers: India's farmers.

Then he set up two plants in Kandla, one for water soluble fertilizers and the other for zinc sulphate, which also dissolves in water. Zinc is one of the essential micronutrients for plants. It is a key constituent of many enzymes and proteins.

'Save the Soil' is an ongoing project. It is part of the annual targets of IFFCO executives. There are other programmes running parallel with 'Save the Soil'.

'We also have Cordet [Cooperative Rural Development Trust], which functions at all our plants. We impart training to farmers and maintain a live museum of horticulture, dairy, poultry, fishery, beekeeping and such activities. There are soil testing laboratories. There are biofertilizer units,' said Yogendra Kumar, Marketing Director, IFFCO.

When farmers come for training, they see for themselves how these activities are carried out. Cordet also handles IFFCO's Integrated Rural Development Programme (IRDP) where it takes up infrastructure development activities like roads, schools, drinking water and other facilities within a radius of 15 kilometres of IFFCO's plants. Every year, an annual budget is sanctioned for the IRDP.

Awasthi's message

IFFCO took off on the wings of autonomy and expansion. Awasthi's message to his colleagues on 1 April 2009 is indicative of the stature and strength IFFCO had acquired by then. He wrote:

> Dear Friends,
>
> The year 2008–2009 has been an exceptional year [...] With your dedication, commitment and devotion, the Society has surpassed all its previous records in the area of Production, Sales, Turnover and Transportation. IFFCO has produced the highest ever 71.68 lakh MT of fertilizers [...] I feel exceedingly happy to inform you that your Society has crossed the landmark sale and transportation of over 112 lakh MT of fertilizer material registering a sharp rise of 20% over the last year. With this, IFFCO has now become the largest marketer of process fertilizers not only in India but in the entire World.
>
> [...]
>
> Under the Vision 2010, your Society was required to achieve Annual Turnover of ₹15,000 crore by the year 2010. You would be delighted to know that your Society has already achieved the Sales Turnover of about ₹32,800 crore during the financial year 2008–2009.
>
> [...]

All these feats have been possible primarily due to our strong commitments to Cooperatives and service to farmers [...] IFFCO Kisan Sanchar Limited (IKSL) has expanded its network in most parts of the country. Its products viz. Kisan Torch and Kisan Lantern are gaining popularity amongst the farmers. IKSL is sending five free voice messages disseminating agricultural related information to about 15 lakh farmers every day. IFFCO-Tokio General Insurance Company (ITGI) [...] is providing insurance cover to the poorest of poor at very nominal premium. Work on IFFCO Kisan SEZ is in full swing. IFFCO Foundation and Indian Farm Forestry Development Cooperative Limited (IFFDC) are also doing very well.

[...]

The Society has bagged the prestigious Economic Times, Acer and Intel Smart Workplace Award in the Manufacturing & Industrial Segment.

[...]

I am confident that IFFCO shall continue its endeavour to achieve still higher goals with your utmost determination and devotion, generosity and blessings of The Almighty, and valuable guidance from the chairman and the board of directors. I am grateful for full support from the Department of Fertilizers and the Ministry of Agriculture and Cooperation.

With regards and good wishes,
U.S. Awasthi

The big picture

'I visualized a larger picture of producing everything a farmer requires under cooperative ownership,' Awasthi said. 'They did not have insurance. There were no agrochemicals for their crops. There was absence of quality seeds. There was no talk of how to make their lands green or how to increase forest cover in the countryside. They did not have information about modern technology. There was no place where they could be trained. We considered all these concerns in our growth plan.'

IFFCO is one of the top cooperatives in the world. In the fertilizer segment, it is ranked as number one. It has emerged as a one-stop shop for farmers for insurance, communication, agro-processing and agrochemicals.

'We have grown because of their support,' said Awasthi.

SIX

SINK OR SWIM

Abhay Oswal was one of India's leading industrialists in the early years of the current millennium. He set up the world's largest integrated factory for phosphatic fertilizers at Paradeep in Odisha in 2001. It was also the world's largest phosphoric acid plant. But the unit had been beset with problems from the beginning. Several attempts to set things right and get it back on track had failed.

The market was rife with rumours that the company had begun defaulting on its debt repayment obligations. Ranjan Sharma, who was then Director, Finance, Oswal Phosphates and Chemicals, said, 'We had considered the option of inviting outside companies to do production on a contract basis. We had discussions with IFFCO and Tata Chemicals on this but could not come to any agreement. The condition of the company kept deteriorating. Then banks restructured the company's debt...'

Meanwhile, IFFCO had realized that it needed a phosphatic fertilizer facility in eastern India. Transporting fertilizers from Kandla to this region was proving to be expensive and this was impacting its profit margins.

Banks wanted to play matchmaker

A senior executive at a multinational bank who had been exposed to the project asked Rakesh Kapur, Joint Managing Director, IFFCO, if he would be interested in taking over Oswal's Odisha plant. Kapur's non-committal reply was, 'We can think about it.'

A few days later, Sharma called to ask for a meeting. In Awasthi's chamber, he tried to give the impression that all was well with the plant. 'These bankers will keep coming to you and try to play matchmaker; but don't be under the impression that we want to sell the plant. We are running it and we will continue running it,' he declared.

This was in keeping with Oswal's frequent declarations that he would replace IFFCO as the numero uno in the Indian fertilizer industry.

Awasthi's response was: 'Fine, don't sell if you don't want to sell.'

But the reality was beginning to bite Oswal. The principal amount outstanding to lenders on account of the Odisha plant was ₹1,800 crore. The outstanding interest was between ₹300 crore and ₹400 crore.

'The banks started putting extreme pressure on us,' said Sharma, who is now managing director of IFFCO Kisan Rural Finance Limited. 'They started asking us for weekly reports. This was unbearable for Abhay Oswal. He realized that the company would not last long. He would lose his reputation in the market and his Shahjahanpur plant would also be in danger. When the banks asked him to consider selling the plant, he agreed.'

The lenders took the proposal to KRIBHCO, which showed interest in acquiring the Paradeep unit. An MOU was signed with it in this regard. It was only at this stage that Awasthi became seriously interested in acquiring the Oswal plant.

Awasthi shows interest

He called Sharma and said, 'Arre, is your plant being sold?'

'Yes,' replied Sharma.

'What will KRIBHCO do with it?'

'You tell me...I thought you were not interested.'

'Arre, why won't I be interested?'

'If you are serious, then I can take the matter ahead,' said Sharma.

'Yes, I am serious,' Awasthi responded and immediately added, 'I am sending Rakesh and Manish to you.'

Things began to move at a rapid pace from this point. Kapur and Gupta met Sharma for lunch within two hours of that telephone call.

Before meeting them, Sharma told his then boss, 'IFFCO is showing interest. I think it will be the right fit for the plant and it will probably pay slightly more than KRIBHCO. But if you talk about it with the others then it will all go wrong.'

Sharma told them that there was nothing fundamentally wrong with the plant or the technology used. It was just being managed badly. 'I also told them that there were some infirmities in the plant that could be corrected with some capital expenditure,' he said.

After the lunch meeting, he returned to his office by 2.30 p.m. At 5.00 p.m. that evening, he received a call from Kapur inviting him to a meeting at Awasthi's residence in an hour.

Sharma reached Awasthi's house around 6.00 p.m. His host greeted him warmly and said, 'You have to get the deal done.'

Sharma could sense that he meant business. He said, 'If you want to get it done through me then you will have to give me a little freedom on pricing.'

Awasthi asked for an indicative price band.

'The deal with KRIBHCO is that it will pay the principal amount of the loan on the plant. The interest component will either be written off by the banks or it will be converted into a fresh loan that Abhay Oswal's Shahjahanpur plant will take care of. Mr Oswal will be very pleased if he gets more than what KRIBHCO is paying,' Sharma said.

'Okay, we will think about it, but you do it fast,' the IFFCO managing director told him.

After the meeting, Sharma again called his boss and said, 'Can we meet right now?'

They met at the Hyatt, where Sharma recounted every detail of his discussion with Awasthi and said, 'We should take this proposal seriously and take a decision quickly.'

He made Oswal promise that he would not use IFFCO's offer as a bargaining chip with KRIBHCO or any other buyer. Armed with this assurance, he proposed that his boss meet Awasthi that very evening.

Deal finalized in one day

Sharma vividly recalls Awasthi arriving for the meeting in a crisp white kurta-pyjama. He did not negotiate much with Abhay Oswal. He only said, 'This is my offer, and this is the final and the last offer. I don't like to negotiate. You are an industrialist. You are much bigger in stature than I am. But as an institution's representative, I am equal to you, and I am making this offer on equal terms. But the decision has to be made today.'

Oswal couldn't believe the speed with which Awasthi was proceeding. 'Don't you want to conduct a due diligence of the plant?' he asked incredulously. 'You have neither seen the plant, nor done the due diligence. Others have been doing it for the past month.'

Awasthi replied, 'Since others have already done it, we do not want to do it. We do not have any plant in the eastern part of the country, so we want to acquire it.'

The final deal value was ₹2,085 crore—enough to pay off all the debts and leave a small amount for Oswal. The next big question was where to find the money to fund this transaction.

The question of money

Speed would be of essence in this transaction. But borrowing money from banks could be a time-consuming affair. A gentleman from ICICI Bank used to visit IFFCO pretty often. Awasthi asked him point blank,

'Are you willing to give me ₹2,000 crore today without asking any further questions?'

Against all odds, ICICI Bank replied in the affirmative and advanced the money without negotiating the terms—those were drawn up later.

'We got the loan at a time when interest rates were at their lowest. They started climbing up soon after that,' remembers R.P. Singh.

The primary contract for the acquisition was signed on 5 September 2005, and it was decided that the final contract would be signed on 17 September 2005. Over this period of close to a fortnight, Oswal grew suspicious—or perhaps suspicions were planted in his mind by vested interests—that Awasthi was not serious about acquiring the plant and that he wanted to scuttle his ongoing talks with KRIBHCO. He said, 'I want some advance payment. This contract is not final from my side unless I get some advance payment.'

He was given ₹50 crore as advance. But Oswal said, 'No, no, this is not sufficient. Tomorrow you may back out from the contract, let this money go down the drain, and scuttle my deal with KRIBHCO.'

'What can we do to convince you of our sincerity?' Awasthi asked.

'You pay me another ₹200 crore in advance.'

'We have no problem paying another ₹200 crore, but we will take possession of the plant tomorrow and you will have no control over it.'

'All right! If you give me ₹200 crore today, I will hand over the plant to you tomorrow,' said Oswal.

The contract was signed at 4.17 p.m. on 17 September 2005, which was deemed to be an auspicious time. The cheque was handed over to Oswal, people clapped, photographs were clicked and Awasthi said, 'Tomorrow you have to handover the plant. You book your plane ticket, go to Paradeep and hand over physical possession of the plant to our people.'

After the signing ceremony at Hyatt, Awasthi and Oswal went to inform the Secretary of the Department of Fertilizers about this contract. From there Oswal went home, and Awasthi went back to his office, where he had asked his senior executives to remain until he returned.

Addressing them, he said, 'We have bought this plant under a strategy. We do not have any plant of complex fertilizers in eastern India. This will strengthen the company's business in eastern and southern India. But this acquisition is also a big challenge for us. We do not have experience in the production of phosphoric acid. We have only been importing phosphoric acid so far. We will have to work very hard to make this acquisition a success. Tomorrow, our team, under the leadership of K.L. Singh [who was then the unit head of IFFCO's mother plant in Kalol], will go to Paradeep and take physical possession of the plant.'

The room burst into spontaneous applause.

An unprecedented development

'This acquisition was an epoch-making event in the history of cooperatives,' said a senior cooperative leader. 'You will recall that it was a period of disinvestments in PSUs. At that time, a farmers' cooperative acquiring a big manufacturing plant from a leading industrialist was a huge achievement. The total credit for this acquisition goes to Dr Awasthi.'

Awasthi had bought the plant without even seeing it because he was confident that he could turn it around. 'We knew it had the world's largest phosphoric acid plant. There were environmental and other issues needed to be tackled. But these were not impossible to resolve,' he said.

The next day, an IFFCO team, under K.L. Singh's leadership, reached Paradeep. They were taken to the guest house where Oswal had asked his senior officers to be present.

After the introductions, the team was taken to the plant at 8.00 p.m. This time was chosen because employees of the day and night shifts would both be present.

Shock at first sight

The first impression was one of shock. What they saw was an old, dilapidated factory that looked like it had been bombarded. Most of the asbestos sheets on the roof were broken. It was drizzling and rainwater was falling on the machines inside the plant. There was waterlogging everywhere. With great difficulty, the IFFCO team walked towards a stage that had been erected, gingerly stepping on bricks placed over the waterlogged grounds. All the workers gathered there were soaked.

Addressing the workers, Oswal said, 'Keeping in mind your interests, I have sold this plant to IFFCO, the country's biggest fertilizer company. All of you will be retained. There will be no retrenchment. You should not worry. I assure all of you that this decision of mine will prove to be better for your future.'

Then, K.L. Singh delivered a small introductory speech seeking everyone's cooperation. IFFCO was now in charge of the plant. The next morning, Oswal left after breakfast. R.P. Singh and a few others stayed back to assist K.L. Singh.

The plant is a 1,500 acre facility on the Cuttack–Paradeep highway. Awasthi launched himself into its revival on a war footing. All the technology suppliers and vendors were immediately contacted. Jacobs from the US was the technology supplier for the phosphoric acid and DAP units. Lurgi, of Germany, had supplied the sulphuric acid technology.

'He would be on the phone, on the mail, on the fax [...] He wrote mails to them to send their engineers immediately to Paradeep. He would keep on taking feedback from the plant through his own channels,' recalls R.P. Singh.

He also asked Mr Kotlarevsky, a former managing director of ICS, Senegal, who had experience in running phosphoric acid plants, to join the operation.

'Essar had been given land in front of our plant. I told the chief minister that this land should be given to us. Mr [Naveen] Patnaik acquiesced. I told him: "Sir, you will be proud of this plant once we revive it,'" adds Awasthi.

Technology suppliers wash their hands of the plant

Awasthi and his team were in for another shock. The condition of the phosphoric acid plant was very poor. It was the world's largest facility with a capacity of 2,650 tonnes a day. But the Jacobs team said it would not be possible to revive it.

'They said straight away that they would not touch the plant,' R.P. Singh recalls.

When K.L. Singh suggested some measures, they said, 'These things cannot be done. We will not recommend even you to do it.'

The team from Lurgi also gave a similar disappointing report about the sulphuric acid plant. They said it would not be possible to run the plant at even half the rated capacity.

One by one, all the experts left. It was a period of extreme stress for Awasthi. Many people began to question his judgement. They said, 'What have you bought? It is total junk. There is nothing in the plant.'

The refrain was reminiscent of his purchase of land in Gurgaon for the IFFCO township. Then, too, people had criticized him for buying what they thought was a worthless piece of land. Then, Awasthi's ability to see beyond the immediate had proved to be a winner. This time, too, he was determined to ensure a similar happy ending. He turned to K.L. Singh to execute his vision.

The plant can run, the plant will run

'I remember the day I went to apprise Dr Awasthi of the situation at Paradeep,' said K.L. Singh. 'He was under great stress during those days. I arrived at about 7.00 p.m. The boardroom was packed with IFFCO's senior executives. I broke the news in one simple sentence. I said, "This plant can run; and this plant will run."'

The whole room reverberated with applause.

Awasthi said, 'K.L. Singh, you can ask for whoever you want.' Then, he turned to the rest. 'Whoever K.L. Singh points to will have to go with him or he will have to resign. If he points towards me, I will have to go and sit there.' Then he asked K.L. Singh how many months he would take to revive the plant.

'It will take long to fully restore the plant,' he said. 'We will first run it to see what the problems are. Then we will prioritize how we will fix them,' he replied. In his mind, he had already worked out a plan. What is a plant after all? It is a combination of many machines. IFFCO was ready to give him all the resources. If he couldn't restore the plant, he would build a new one.

The biggest problem he faced was a shortage of people with experience in phosphoric acid, remembers R.P. Singh. Actually, it wasn't a shortage; there was literally no one.

Awasthi said, 'Let's look at retired IFFCO people.'

The company trawled through data on all its retired personnel and selected fifty people. Happily, all of them agreed to come on board for the project.

IFFCO had booked two hotels near the plant at very reasonable rates for the entire year to accommodate its visiting employees, as well as the foreign consultants from Jacobs and Lurgi and people like Mr Kotlarevsky. It had also signed long-term contracts for transportation. Suddenly 40–50 Innova and Scorpio cars appeared in Paradeep. Everything was happening at breakneck speed.

The K.L. Singh-led team also had to resolve or work its way around a host of other problems. There were problems with the design of the equipment. There were problems with drainage as Paradeep is a high-rainfall area. There was the issue of disposal of phospho-gypsum, which is a pollutant. The challenge was how to tackle the problems in a manner that did not affect the environment.

Workers turn hostile

But the most difficult, surprising and shocking problem was that of the workers turning hostile. 'This wasn't something we had anticipated,' said Awasthi. 'Under the previous management, they were not even getting their salaries fully or on time. We told them on the very first day that they would be properly paid.' IFFCO even increased their salaries across the board to bring them at par with its pay scales at its other plants.

R.P. Singh said, 'We retained all those who wanted to work. But I found that within the Oswal Group, there was a set of employees who were against this takeover. Maybe they were getting more advantages under the old system. They created problems for us.'

Whole plant in turmoil

Several other unpleasant surprises lay in store for K.L. Singh when he got down to work. Everything was in a state of chaos—the boiler was running, but it was not registered; the authorities had not been paid for electricity; water was being taken from a canal, but payments were overdue; the vehicles in the premises were not registered…there seemed to be a crisis lurking in every corner.

Soon, K.L. Singh's office was flooded with letters from various departments demanding the payment of dues. Then, the plant's HR policies were a mess. There seemed to be as many salary grades as there were employees. And those who had kept the previous owner happy had been given higher salaries and positions.

The good thing was that all the employees were young—most were between twenty-five and thirty-five years of age. But the problem was that almost all of them had come through recommendations; they did not have professional qualifications.

For example, it emerged that when the Directorate of Boilers was approached for registration, its officers had asked for jobs for their relatives; these people had been employed. This pattern was repeated with the Regional Transport Office and several other authorities. This is how most of the recruitments had been made.

Factory submerged

When the rains came, pouring sheets of water, the whole plant was submerged as it did not have a drainage system. Electrical equipment, on which not even a drop of water was meant to fall, were submerged in water. Even the transformers went underwater.

K.L. Singh raised the motor control centres, which control the performance of electrical motors, as high as possible to prevent them from drowning. He also had metre-high platforms built for every transformer.

One day, a platform crashed from a height of about 30 metres. A person had been standing on it. Luckily, he survived because the flooring was not RCC, so he fell on the mud floor. To his utter dismay, K.L. Singh discovered that there was no first-aid system in the plant. 'I immediately appointed a doctor and two to three nurses, and set up a makeshift hospital with an ambulance,' he said.

New problems kept cropping up every day. This phosphoric acid plant was the largest in the world. But every time it would make half the rated amount, one of the tanks would invariably spring a leak and spill the acid into the drain.

Then, a 1.5 kilometre pipeline would carry the sulphuric acid from one tank to another. At any given time, these held 400 tonnes of acid. If it sprung a leak—as it seemed to do with unerring regularity—the 400 tonnes of acid had to be drained out before repairs could begin.

'All the acid used to flow down the drain before our eyes. We went to the plant wearing gumboots, which often got stuck in the mud; so, we had to leave them there,' K.L. Singh remembers with a smile.

Limping back to a semblance of normalcy

It took him three months to locate all the problems—and to figure out what he needed to do, what was urgent and what could wait. It took him three more months to fix the problems temporarily and start production at low capacity. Gradually, the IFFCO team began to get the plant back on its feet. In three years, it started operating at 60–70 per cent of its capacity.

The workers, though, remained hostile. K.L. Singh tried to address their problems by creating grades among them on the basis of their experience and qualifications and doubled their salaries. But they were not satisfied. They wanted more.

Then, there were contract workers who wanted to become permanent. They would create all sorts of disturbances. They would say unspeakable things to his face. They even cut the power supply to K.L. Singh's house several times. But he tolerated everything silently.

A permanent solution

'When we entered the third year of operations, I thought the time had come to address this problem,' said K.L. Singh. 'If I had left without solving it, then people would have thought the management was weak. I decided to resolve this issue in such a way that whoever came after me would not face any problem. And the opportunity came soon.'

Early one morning, as he was preparing to go to work, he received news that the workers were planning to assault him that day. His informer told him not to go to the plant. But he thought: 'I am the captain of this ship. How can I abandon it? It's a high-risk plant. It will be rudderless without me.' He informed the police and went to his office.

At 10.30 a.m., a crowd of about 2,000 people gathered and started heading towards the control rooms, beating up people on the way. Soon, the whole plant was running without any operators or engineers.

It was a terrifying situation. A big accident could have taken place and set off an explosion of catastrophic proportions. A lesser man would have lost his nerve, but K.L. Singh kept his wits about him. 'I called a maintenance engineer from my mobile phone and told him to trip the turbogenerator; this would snap the power supply and bring the whole plant to a standstill,' he said.

His heart was beating fast as he waited for news from his subordinate. Those few moments were terrifying. Luckily for everyone, the maintenance engineer called to say he had done as instructed. 'I can't describe the relief I felt. The plant was safe. Now, I had to decide how to handle the mob marching towards my office,' said K.L. Singh.

The mob was a mixed group of permanent and contract workers and some local criminals who thought they could loot the plant if it shut down. 'There had been cases in the past when plant heads had been brutally assaulted. It had happened during Oswal's time. Militant workers had cut off the hands of one plant head. They had also chopped off the ears of an officer in another incident. That day, they were coming to do something similar to me.'

Those were very tense moments. 'I was in a fix. I saw death coming towards me. I thought I should attack them before they attacked me and ordered the security team to start firing. First, they fired in the air, but that had no impact. Then they straightened their barrels and fired into the mob. A stampede broke out at once,' K.L. Singh informs, reliving those harrowing moments in his mind.

The mob was stunned as they had not anticipated this strong

retaliation. There was chaos as the mob ran helter-skelter for their lives. In less than half an hour, the crowd had completely dissolved.

Fortunately, there were no major casualties. Some people sustained minor injuries in the melee. 'Our purpose was to disperse the mob and send the message that we could take extreme measures if we were forced to. The message reached home squarely. I taught them such a lesson that they would never again dare to do something like that. Since that day, there hasn't been a single disturbance. The plant has been absolutely peaceful,' said K.L. Singh.

He had taken care to keep the local administration in the loop about his plans. A small police force had been present on the scene and had witnessed everything first hand. Since the workers had a reputation for being volatile, the authorities were very supportive of his actions.

When communications resumed with the union leaders, K.L. Singh put forth the condition that they would first have to apologize; only then could talks take place. By then, the workers had realized that the management was ready to take them head on. They apologized and admitted that the path they had taken was wrong. 'I assured them that we would not hold any grudges against them and would work in the best interests of everyone in the plant. The next day, everything was normal and peaceful.'

Soon afterwards, Awasthi recalled K.L. Singh to Delhi. Awasthi said, 'You suggest your successor's name. We now require you at the head office.' Awasthi then created the position of Director, Technical, and appointed him to that post.

That was in 2008. Since then, there has been no disturbance at the Paradeep unit. IFFCO has five plants in the country. The Paradeep plant, which runs at more than 100 per cent capacity utilization, alone generates double the combined profits of the other four plants.

'This plant offers so much flexibility. You can buy rock phosphate and produce phosphoric acid here. You can buy sulphur and produce sulphuric acid. You can produce DAP. You can produce NPK. The port is barely a kilometre away. There is a long train of conveyors that brings materials from the port to the plant. And it is so strategically located—it allows us to easily service all of eastern and southern India,' said K.L. Singh.

An IFFCO insider calls Paradeep another masterstroke by Awasthi. He had the foresight, prescience and determination to turn this toxic asset, which was hollow from inside, into a miracle, he said.

SEVEN

THE PEAK OF THE COOPERATION

By the end of the first decade of the twenty-first century, Awasthi had already established himself as one of the leading international figures in both the fertilizer and cooperative sectors. He had transformed a relatively small fertilizer company into a multinational with a presence in Africa, Oman, Jordan, Dubai and elsewhere. His voice was heard with respect and his decisions often had an impact on many policymakers around the world.

'Yes, indeed. Dr Awasthi is an international figure. I have attended meetings and seminars of IFA and International Cooperative Alliance (ICA) with him. He commands tremendous respect. His opinions matter and people listen to him. We had gone to Kyrgyzstan in 2018. There, he made two announcements. First, that IFFCO and National Cooperative Union of India (NCUI) together would adopt five cooperative societies there and develop them, and second, a soil testing laboratory would be set up there' said Chandrapal Singh Yadav, Chairman, KRIBHCO.

He thinks Awasthi's greatest quality is his capacity to lead from the front. He particularly admires his knack of working with and convincing politicians and bureaucrats about his ideas.

'Getting them to agree with him is an exceptional ability of his,' he said.

Global champion of farmers' interests

Between 2008 and 2009, the IFFCO Foundation organized three international conferences of farmers from Latin America, the Caribbean and South Asian Association for Regional Cooperation countries in collaboration with the Ministry of Agriculture and the Ministry of External Affairs, Government of India, and the Indian Council of Agricultural Research. All the three conferences were held in Delhi. Former Union Minister Suresh Prabhu contributed immensely in its success.

'We thought we should create a platform where farmers from all over the world could come together,' said Suresh Prabhu.

The first conference took place in March 2008. Farmers from South Asian countries participated in this. The theme of the conference was 'Science-based Agricultural Transformation towards Eradication of Poverty and Hunger.' The second conference was held in November 2008 with the theme 'India–Africa Cooperation for Sustainable Food Security.' The third conference was held in November 2009 with the theme 'Cooperation for Food Security in India, Latin America and the Caribbean.'

Following the success of these conferences, the idea of creating an international forum for farmers emerged and the Global Forum for Farmers was established.

Globalizing at a fast pace

IFFCO had, meanwhile, invested in a JV in Jordan to produce phosphoric acid and acquired the rights to mine rock phosphate in Queensland in Australia in its quest to become self-sufficient in the raw materials it needed to manufacture phosphatic fertilizers in India.

'They are not isolated developments. The raw materials that are required to make fertilizers are not available in our country. There aren't sufficient quantities of phosphoric acid, rock phosphate, potash or natural gas in India,' said the IFFCO managing director.

IFFCO was the first in the cooperative sector—and, perhaps, even in India—to establish a JV for phosphoric acid in Africa way back in 1983–1984. It had to take on many partners as it could not make the huge investment it needed on its own. The Senegal plant was the first step towards ensuring raw material security for IFFCO.

Then, it set up a urea plant in Oman. But phosphoric acid supplies were still a matter of concern. International traders were exploiting IFFCO and other Indian buyers. So, it invested in a phosphoric acid plant in Jordan in 2007.

'It was located in a desert. There was no habitation within a radius of 300 kilometres of the plant. We were operating the plant at more than 100 per cent capacity. Then, we realized we were running up a huge import bill but lacked the required expertise in international trade,' said Manish Gupta.

IFFCO lacked the nimble-footedness needed in international trade—and was operating through middlemen. 'Therefore, we set up Kisan International Trading in Dubai. Today, we handle our imports on our own by hedging our foreign exchange exposure and procuring our requirements at the least possible price,' said Awasthi.

Australian tie-up turns sour

IFFCO set out to mine rock phosphate in Australia to secure this crucial raw material for its Paradeep plant. But its relationship with its partner, Legend International Holdings, turned sour very soon. IFFCO had a minority stake in the JV and so it couldn't enforce its writ straight away. When the relationship broke down, it took its partner to court.

'The promoter of Legend had mala fide intentions. We were able to establish that he had defrauded us. We won the case both in Australia and the US and got him declared bankrupt. At present, proceedings are on to recover the money,' said Manish Gupta.

Suppliers offer better terms

But just as every cloud has a proverbial silver lining, this project, too, brought IFFCO some advantage. When IFFCO announced its deal with Legend for the supply of rock phosphate from Australia in 2008 the whole world suddenly seemed keen to supply rock phosphate on very competitive terms.

'Before this deal, everybody used to say "No!" They knew we desperately needed 2 million tonnes of rock phosphate every year. So, their first response would be negative. Then, they would force us to pay high prices for low-quality rocks. But when we announced the Legend deal, every country began offering us good deals,' said Awasthi.

Today, IFFCO gets a regular supply of rocks from Jordan. 'The Jordan partnership happened because of the threat they saw from Australia. They thought, "Let's get IFFCO on our side before Australia does." So, the bad investment resulted in the world opening up for us,' said Awasthi with a laugh.

Canada project on hold

IFFCO wanted to expand its capacity. When the expansion was conceived in 2011, the price of urea was about $500 per tonne. When all the preliminary work ended after about two years, urea prices started crashing and came down to $170 per tonne.

'At this lower price it is not viable to set up a urea plant. We tried some other options, but finally scrapped the project,' said Manish Gupta.

Awasthi adds: 'Fertilizer is our DNA. No matter how much we do other things, we are ultimately a fertilizer company. And we should manufacture more fertilizers because there is a shortage in the country. We still import about 30 per cent of our requirements every year.'

IFFCO's foreign JVs, therefore, have to be seen through the lens of India's food security.

'The Oman plant has given us more than all our plants in India combined. The margins are very small in India. That was why we began exploring the option of setting up plants outside the country. We went to Senegal before anyone else. Then, we went to Oman and Jordan. The Legend story is a part of that vision,' explains Awasthi.

New subsidy formula shakes up industry

The government radically altered the formula for paying fertilizer subsidies in 2010. 'The pay out was getting scandalously high,' said Atul Chaturvedi, former Secretary, Department of Fertilizers. 'When I took charge of the department on 27 July 2008, the subsidy was more than ₹1 lakh crore.'

When he studied the issue in detail, he found the prices of end-fertilizers were fixed while the amount of the subsidies kept fluctuating. After much deliberation, Chaturvedi proposed that the subsidy be fixed on the nutrients; the end-prices would fluctuate under this system.

This was a radical departure from the existing practice. When Chaturvedi discussed the idea with the industry, he received mixed responses. The efficient players came out in favour of the proposal, but those enjoying protection under the existing regime opposed the idea. The main problem was with the urea industry.

The Union Cabinet cleared the nutrient-based formula, called the Nutrient Based Subsidy (NBS) scheme, for phosphate and potash but said it would decide on nitrogen (urea) later. That 'later' never materialized. Urea remains under the old product-based subsidy regime.

'The NBS scheme is a step towards decontrol of fertilizers, which we have been demanding for a long time,' Awasthi informs. 'The Retention Price Scheme has become obsolete now. The time has come for a change...but for reasons I am not aware of, the scheme was not implemented for urea.'

The government has taken other steps, such as neem-coating, to prevent diversion. But urea use remains rampant because of its ridiculously low price.

'This is destroying our soil. I have always said this problem can only be corrected by direct transfer of subsidies to farmers,' said Awasthi.

The existing subsidy structure gives small and marginal farmers, who make up 82 per cent of the farmer population, only 39 per cent of the total subsidy pay out. Big and wealthy farmers, accounting for just 18 per cent of farmers in the country, corner 61 per cent of the cake. This defeats the very purpose of giving subsidies.

'When I met Prime Minister Narendra Modi in December 2014, I requested him to give subsidies directly to the farmers. Let the industry compete with international manufacturers. Let the farmer decide how he wishes to buy fertilizers. It will usher in a market for consumers rather than producers. It will also force farmers to use fertilizers more cautiously and judiciously,' said Awasthi, forever the champion of farmers' interests.

The NBS scheme forced Indian companies to step out of their protected cocoons in the complex fertilizer segment. Now, they have to anticipate customers' preferences. They have to be conscious of the moves of their competitors. They have to be on their toes.

'I do not wish to take credit, but IFFCO showed how it could negotiate a better deal for itself in the international market. We brought down the price of DAP from $570 per tonne to $500 per tonne in our deal with the supplier,' he informs.

That agreement was signed in the presence of the then Prime Ministers of India and Russia, Dr Manmohan Singh and Vladimir Putin. Awasthi signed it on behalf of IFFCO and IPL. The deal was for the supply of 1 million tonnes of DAP per year for a period of three years (2010–2013). It ensured the supply price was maintained within the broad contours of the NBS scheme. The Government of India saved ₹1,500 crore to ₹1,600 crore on its subsidy bill over those three years.

Focus on neem oil

'We started the production of neem oil in Phulpur. When Prime Minister Modi announced that urea would be neem-coated to prevent diversion, Dr Awasthi started the plantation of neem trees on a war footing,' said Yogendra Kumar, Marketing Director, IFFCO.

The company planted 1.2 crore neem trees in 2021–2022. 'We are also doing a research project with the Forest Research Institute, Dehradun, to develop a new species of neem that matures faster and contains more oil. The results are very encouraging. Six neem varieties have been developed and patented as FRI-IFFCO 1 to 6,' Kumar adds.

Venturing into agrochemicals

Ashok Yadav, a director at IFFCO, told Awasthi sometime in 2013, 'Our product range has one missing component—agrochemicals. If you bring agrochemicals to the market, it will really help the farmers.'

The IFFCO managing director thought this was a very good suggestion. At that time, the market was full of fake products that were being sold at exorbitant prices. Farmers, too, were clamouring for IFFCO to launch agrochemicals that would protect their crops.

'India's farmers need proper chemicals at affordable prices to protect their crops. There used to be anarchy in the market before we entered. The farmers were confused. The same product was being sold at different prices at different places,' informs Awasthi.

Said A. Roy, Managing Director, IFFCO-MC Crop Science: 'We had fertilizers. We had seeds. There was a persistent demand from farmers that we should also introduce agrochemicals.'

In the same year, Awasthi told him that he had decided to enter the agrochemical segment. IFFCO had ample room at all its plants to manufacture agrochemicals. But it had no idea how the agrochemical industry worked.

The team set up by Awasthi met consultants and experts for advice. It found that Mitsubishi Corporation traded in agrochemicals. The team was familiar with the Mitsubishi Group. IFFCO's insurance partner, Tokio Marine, is a Mitsubishi Group company.

The Japanese company suggested IFFCO prepare a feasibility report. A professional consultant engaged for the purpose gave a very encouraging report. It was still a relatively untapped area. Cooperative societies, which are IFFCO's most important distribution channel, had kept out of this business as they did not trust the private players that were then selling agrochemicals.

In a happy coincidence, Mitsubishi had been looking for a partner in India. The two companies decided to join hands. They formed a JV called IFFCO-MC Crop Science in August 2015. IFFCO holds 51 per cent equity in the company and Mitsubishi Corporation the balance 49 per cent.

Awasthi deputed a management team from IFFCO; they were given specific instructions on how to manage the new business. He kept monitoring the progress of the new company till it could stand on its own, and he moved on to other projects only after that. This was in keeping with his philosophy of always moving from one project to another for the benefit of India's farmers.

'We entered the market with generic products because new products require rigorous field trials. It's a long process that takes five to six years. We first wanted to get a feel of the market. We could expand our range later,' said Roy.

IFFCO designed a transparent model and fixed the prices of its agro-chemicals throughout the country. Channel partners, mostly cooperative societies, were offered a fixed margin. This ensured a fixed MRP for farmers.

But marketing proved to be very challenging. IFFCO had a field force of 500 agricultural scientists deployed all over the country at different levels. But they were not familiar with agrochemicals.

So IFFCO set up a knowledge team of about hundred regional

marketing executives in IFFCO-MC to provide technical support to the sales team. 'We also started intensive training programmes for our field people. Now, they are qualified to guide the farmers,' said Roy.

The team found that farmers tend to apply more than the required quantities of agrochemicals without any care for timing and proportions. The company organized meetings with farmers and explained to them how and in what quantities they should apply these chemicals.

'Our philosophy is different from that of other sellers in the market. We handhold farmers to the extent possible. Our job does not finish with selling the product. We tell them when to apply, how to apply and in what proportions to apply agrochemicals,' Awasthi informs.

There was a crop failure in Punjab in 2015 as the timing of the application of weedicides was wrong. Usually, the temperature falls after wheat is sown. But the temperature did not fall that year; it remained high for an extended period. The prescribed method was to spray weedicide after the first irrigation. The weeds sprout when the temperature falls. Farmers applied the weedicide even though the temperature had remained high. The mercury finally dipped after a month, but by then the weedicide had lost its efficacy; Weeds destroyed the crop.

'That's why training is essential. We have conducted exhaustive training programmes involving our people, cooperative societies and farmers. It's an ongoing process,' said the IFFCO-MC chief.

In the early years, Awasthi used to monitor the outcomes of these training sessions. Any complaint from the farmers or the cooperatives was immediately addressed.

'This is where we are different from others. He never compromises on that. Farmers and their interests are sacrosanct. That has been his guiding principle,' adds Roy.

The decision to enter the agrochemical segment proved prescient as the company earned a profit in the first year itself.

Year-long golden jubilee celebrations

IFFCO completed fifty years of its existence in 2017. The year-long celebrations stood out for two major initiatives—Awasthi's pan-India travels, called Kisan Sahkar Janyatra, to 125 locations, and the launch of the Indian Cooperative Digital Platform (ICDP).

The IFFCO managing director, then seventy-two years old, maintained a furious pace, covering all these locations, giving speeches, meeting people, while simultaneously running the world's largest fertilizer cooperative. Most people had thought he would not be able to visit all the locations. But not for the first time, he belied all apprehensions and proved everyone wrong.

Varanasi was his 125th pit stop. The function was held in BHU, Awasthi's alma mater, bang opposite the Department of Chemical Engineering, where he had earned his degree. The chief executives of all the IFFCO subsidiaries, as well as several senior and mid-level IFFCO executives, were in attendance. A stream of farmers made up the rest of the audience of about 2,000 people.

Addressing the gathering, he said:

> Dear Brothers and Sisters,
>
> Varanasi is the last destination of our year-long journey, which we started to celebrate fifty years of IFFCO. We have been able to successfully complete these fifty years because of your love, support and blessings. So, it was our bounden duty to come to you and express our gratitude from the bottom of our heart…
>
> I travelled across the country and visited 125 locations—from Arunachal to Kutch and from Andaman to Leh—and found our farmers are the same everywhere. They all face the same problems. The same problem also afflicts all our cooperative societies…
>
> I remember I joined this university in 1962. It was a difficult period for our country. Our food production capacity was very

meagre. We had begged America for wheat and got it under the PL-480 programme. It was a terrible time. I vividly remember how people used to wait for the wheat to reach the port. It was a ship-to-mouth scenario. It was at that precarious time that China attacked India. It was then that I decided I would join a profession where I would be able to do something for India's farmers...

In my year-long journey, I have seen that there are many pockets in our country where farmers and cooperative societies have combined and brought about tremendous growth in their production. They have done it themselves, without any outside support...

You, too, can do it. Times have changed. Technology has brought opportunities to your doorstep. That's why wherever we have gone, we have tried to make people aware of technology and made efforts to deliver them its benefits...

Farmers and cooperatives are our soul. We work to nourish that soul...we always think about you, about how we can make your lives better...you are our masters...we seek your continued blessings and affection.

Thank you.

Digital technology can change the face of rural India

'The twenty-first century is the century of digital technology. When Prime Minister Modi announced the Digital India initiative, we thought it was a golden opportunity for us to work on using technology to improve the lot of farmers and generate incomes and prosperity in rural India,' said Awasthi.

IFFCO had the capacity and the reach to do it—it had 36,000 cooperative societies as its members and was connected with more than five crore farmers across the country. In 2017, Awasthi discussed the matter with the board of directors and decided that IFFCO would interact with its member societies, member farmers and even those farmers who were not connected to it, and bring them on board its proposed technology platform. The IFFCO team would invite them to its meetings, take care of their travel, food and lodging, and explain to them how the platform could transform their lives.

'We launched the ICDP in thirteen languages together. The idea was more communication, more knowledge and more knowledge sharing,' said Awasthi.

A.K. Gupta, General Manager, IT Services, IFFCO, said, 'I remember the first meeting that Dr Awasthi called to discuss the idea. All the directors and the senior executives of IFFCO were present. He described his vision. He said all our group companies would also be part of it. But he set an impossible deadline. He said he wanted the portal to be ready in three days.'

The Director, IT, said that such portals take a minimum of six months to set up, but Awasthi dismissed his plea saying, 'I will be on tour. Rakesh Kapur will be around. He will launch the portal on the fourth day. This is final and there will be no change.'

He had selected twelve young professionals from IFFCO, its JVs and other subsidiaries, and assigned them the work. He said, 'I have constituted a young team that will make this portal.' Gupta was appointed the leader of this team.

Gupta and his team developed the portal in three days and it was launched by Rakesh Kapur on the fourth day. It was a very basic portal. When Awasthi returned from tour and saw their handiwork, he rejected it outright.

'Change it completely,' he ordered.

The team was at its wits' end. It didn't know what to do. The HR director saved the day with his suggestion. 'Gupta, you have to be fast and perfect; you will have to outsource this work to professionals. There are many new-generation start-ups. Find one with experience in handling rural projects,' he said.

Gupta located Loco Vida, a three-year-old company in Delhi with a small team of twenty-five people that had done some rural projects. 'We moved fast and signed them on, and the next morning our work started. The portal was ready within a week,' he said.

But Awasthi was a difficult boss to please. He said, 'You are going in the right direction. But this portal is in English. I want it in all the local languages of the country.' This was another challenge.

Awasthi wanted to showcase this technology portal at the golden jubilee meetings he was holding around the country. That meant Gupta's team would have to simultaneously develop thirteen web portals. Any change in one language would lead to changes in all the portals.

'We got all the pages synced. Our executives from various states vetted the language and we were good to go,' said Gupta.

Then, Awasthi wanted a call centre developed to answer queries from visitors to the portal. 'We should be able to handle queries in all the local languages. If a query in a local language is answered in English, then it does not serve any purpose,' he said.

By this time, Awasthi's young team had started to fall into lockstep with their boss's near-impossible deadlines. When a few experts said it would take a minimum of two months to set up such a call centre, Gupta and his team weren't particularly perturbed.

'We wanted the call centre up and running in a week's time. Our partner, Tokio Marine, runs call centres in forty-two countries. When I discussed the idea with them, they said that they could set it up in a month,' recalls Gupta, adding that he told them to compress that timeline into one week.

'That's impossible. We can try to do it in fifteen days.'

And that was it!

Gupta and his team settled all the commercial terms and called Awasthi for permission. He asked, 'Are you taking care of all the languages?'

'Yes, Sir.'

'Go, ahead.'

The contract was signed on a Saturday. The recruitments were done the next day. Two days were spent on training and, on Wednesday, a full-fledged IFFCO call centre went live. The first call came around 1.00 p.m. that very afternoon.

The customer support number is 1800-183-1967. The last four digits represent IFFCO's birth year.

It was sheer teamwork and trust that allowed Gupta's team to beat the seemingly impossible deadlines and deliver the project on time, The joint managing director, the finance director and other senior executives readily approved what Gupta negotiated. Everything was processed and approved within a day. Gupta gave them the work order for two years.

When the portal and the call centre started operations, the marketing director said, 'Let's start e-commerce now.'

By this time, the traffic to the website had started rising. 'We synchronized with IFFCO eBazar to take care of deliveries. At first, there were very limited orders,' said Gupta.

Initially, the portal handled orders only from Haryana. It faced the usual teething problems, like product inadequacy, imperfect packaging and delayed deliveries.

IFFCO's Director, Joint Venture & Strategy, Manish Gupta, suggested that the e-commerce platform should find a logistics partner. His idea was that all the products on offer should be available with that partner and the processing of orders should be automatic, so that these could be shipped directly to customers.

This was done and the glitches were ironed out.

Then Awasthi said, 'I want this facility for the entire country.'

IFFCO tied up with a logistics partner that could cater to 13,000 pin codes across the country and launched its pan-India e-commerce services. Initially, it set a minimum ticket size of ₹399.

Awasthi shot this down, saying, 'There will be no minimum order size for our farmers. Even if the order is for ₹10, we will deliver that free of cost to his doorstep.'

The minimum ticket size condition was dropped, and the market response improved.

In his meetings with farmers across India, Awasthi popularized the idea, and the team demonstrated how the portal could be accessed and orders placed. He did this in 125 locations across the length and breadth of India and he met 1,500–2,000 farmers at each place.

The team also made a film which was screened at all the meetings about how farmers could very easily place orders digitally and get their needs delivered to their houses. The film was made in all the regional languages. Social media platforms, like Twitter, Facebook and WhatsApp, were used extensively to spread awareness about the initiative. Also, the extensive coverage of the golden jubilee celebrations in print and electronic media helped popularize the idea.

The objective behind holding the golden jubilee celebrations all over the country was to sensitize farmers about balanced fertilization and modern techniques of farming, informs Awasthi.

Once the portal and the e-commerce platform were up and running, the team at IFFCO began to brainstorm on how to widen their scope of operations. They realized that one important way could be to create opportunities for farmers to do business. Secondly, the platform could be used to reduce their cost of production. Third, they could tell them how to produce a good crop. And lastly, the link could be used to educate farmers on how to ensure good health of their soil so that they could get higher yields.

These were the ideas that inspired the launch of ICDP. It was not named IFFCO Cooperative Digital Platform because Awasthi wanted farmers from everywhere—members and non-members—to make the platform their own.

More than 2.5 crore farmers became members of the digital platform during the year-long golden jubilee campaign. 'It's a complete hub for farmers—soil management, seeds, weather, rates in the mandis, new diseases and their cures, the various central and state government schemes…All the information is available,' said the IFFCO chief.

ICDP operates in thirteen languages. There is instant translation. Farmers who communicate in one language can interact with farmers who use other languages in real time. The call centres work twenty-four seven to provide uninterrupted support. All a farmer has to do is type www.iffcobazar.in to connect to the digital platform. He has to fill his name, address and mobile number to become a member of ICDP.

There are still no big players in the agriculture-related e-commerce business, so there is vast scope for this business to expand.

Grand finale, grand spectacle

With this, he brought the curtain down on the year-long Kisan Sahkar Janyatra. The final act in this year-long story would be the grand finale at IFFCO's mother plant in Kalol on 3 November 2017.

'The grand finale was a spectacle to showcase the fifty years of IFFCO,' said Apoorva, who was part of the core team Awasthi had put together to organize the function. Guests were expected from all over the world. Awasthi's brief to the team was simple: nothing less than a world-class function would be acceptable.

Initially, several VVIPs expressed their inability to attend citing prior engagements. Awasthi wrote personal letters, telling each one of them, 'I want you to attend the function.' All of them replied that they would do so. He also called some of them and got them to agree to come.

Mitsubishi Corporation (Japan) wrote to say it would take care of the accommodation of its representatives. Awasthi immediately instructed his team to write back saying, 'No, you are our guests. We will take care of your accommodation.'

The company booked more than two hundred rooms for its guests in Hyatt, and about seventy more in Crown Plaza, both in Ahmedabad. Initially, it had not booked any suites, but as the date of the function drew closer, it had to book an additional twenty suites at the Hyatt.

Awasthi stayed in the director's bungalow in Kalol. He said, 'I will not stay in Hyatt. You people will take care of Hyatt. I will stay at the location to oversee the preparations.'

A Russian delegation from ICA wanted to meet Awasthi on the morning of 3 November, the day of the grand finale. The team members were sure the request would be turned down. They, nevertheless, conveyed the message to Awasthi. To their utter surprise, he agreed to see the delegation. 'Ask them to come at 9.00 a.m.. I will meet them,' he said.

The delegation reached the director's bungalow at the appointed hour. Awasthi met them for forty-five minutes and took them to the unveiling of the Golden Jubilee Column, which was to happen soon, at 10.00 a.m.

'This shows how easily he manages time,' said Madhavi, another member of the core team with unabashed admiration. 'He also remembered the names of all the VIPs who were there at the function. There were times when I would tell him that such and such persons are not on the list, and he would say, "Look carefully," and those persons would invariably be there.'

The dinner at the grand finale was held at the Hyatt. Awasthi personally planned the seating arrangements for the two hundred guests who had been invited. On every table, there was a member of the IFFCO family or its representative. Plaques bearing the names of the guests were placed in their assigned places at the tables.

Awasthi personally welcomed all the guests and also went around all the tables to meet them. He had planned everything—from their entry, to seating, to exit—to the last detail, which were meticulously executed.

The photographs of all the thirty-eight VVIPS who had been honoured were framed and presented to them. All the two hundred VIPs were sent beautifully designed pen drives that contained videos and photographs of the event.

The awards and honours were followed by a reading of a message from the Prime Minister Modi on IFFCO's golden jubilee celebrations. Then, Awasthi delivered his speech:

> Respected Chairman Sir, honourable guests, ladies, gentlemen and our farmer brethren who have come here in multitudes,
>
> Our history of fifty years, if we start counting them, then it is a huge time period. Fifty years is a long, long period. But if we are standing here today, if we are celebrating today, then it has entirely been possible because of the farmers and cooperatives in the country. We have grown with their support. Their love, affection and trust have been our nourishment in this journey of fifty years…
>
> Today I wish to remember our first Chairman, Maharaj Uday Bhan Singh Ji. He visualized what could be the difference between a cooperative society and professional management and all our other chairmen followed it religiously. I also wish to remember our first Managing Director Padma Shri Paul Pothen. The ethics he laid down for professional management became our guide.
>
> Dear friends, time changes very fast. What was yesterday is not present today. What is today will not be there tomorrow. What will be tomorrow will be obsolete after five years. So, we have to remain technologically agile. Our eyes are focused on the sky and our feet are rooted to the ground but our hearts throb for the farmers and the cooperatives. As long as we uphold this value nothing in this world can stop our onward march. We will keep moving ahead scaling new heights.
>
> Thank you.

The whole audience gave Awasthi a standing ovation.

The finale was a heady mix of technology and culture. It was a five-hour medley of songs and dances interspersed with the story of IFFCO.

Shankar Mahadevan and Shreya Ghoshal were selected to record the song, '*Mitti ki Jaan, Kisan ki Shaan*'.

The song was recorded in twelve regional languages. It was a huge task. It meant finding twelve male singers, twelve female singers, twelve translators and lyricists and background singers for each language. H.S. Vardhan, Head of Public Relations, gives full credit for this to R.K. Swamy BBDO, the agency hired for the purpose.

Along with IFFCO, Awasthi, too, completed 50 years in the fertilizer industry that year. A short audio-visual capturing the golden moments of his professional life was presented towards the end of the programme.

The evening concluded with a spectacular display of fireworks.

Professional management, diverse board

IFFCO had humble beginnings, with fifty-seven members and a capital of ₹5 lakh. 'The evolution and growth of the company from that small beginning into such a huge enterprise is our greatest achievement,' said Awasthi.

The way IFFCO is run is unique. The management is professional, and the board of directors have people from diverse backgrounds, including politics, cooperatives, agriculture and other fields. The professional body managing the society is answerable to the board and works under its guidance. This distinction between the management and the board is the hallmark of IFFCO.

'Never has the professional management tried to influence the election of board members. Similarly, the elected board has never interfered with the professional management. This healthy tradition has enabled IFFCO to scale new heights [...] We have proved that a democratically elected, self-governing cooperative society based on voluntary participation is a wonderful model of management,' said Awasthi with visible pride.

A quiet start

The IFFCO story started in 1962–1963 when chemical fertilizers were first being used in India. Cooperative societies were the main distribution channel for these fertilizers. But they did not have their own manufacturing unit.

CLUSA suggested that a fertilizer plant be set up under cooperative ownership in India, and asked ACDI/VOCA to make a project report. That project report led to the formation of IFFCO.

IFFCO was registered as a multi-state cooperative society on 3 November 1967 under the Bombay Cooperative Societies Act. Two plants were set up—in Kalol for ammonia and urea, and in Kandla for DAP/NPK. Both these plants are in Gujarat.

'Production started in 1975 and since then, IFFCO has regularly been paying dividends. Today, it has twenty-two subsidiary and allied companies. But despite its current size and diversification away from fertilizers, farmers and cooperatives have remained IFFCO's soul. It never lost focus—its order of priorities, according to its chief executive, is farmers, cooperatives and the human resources of the company,' Awasthi said, adding, 'We have been able to reach here because of the cooperation and the mutual trust between these three components.'

A lifeline for cooperatives

Awasthi's contribution to keeping the cooperative movement in India in good health is widely acknowledged. A large organization like the Pradeshik Cooperative Federation is able to pay salaries to its employees because of the dividends it receives from IFFCO.

'I am chairman of the State Cooperative Federation of Uttarakhand. We have shares of ₹30 crore in IFFCO on which we get a dividend of ₹6 crore every year,' said Pramod Kumar Singh.

Three hundred employees get their salaries out of this money. That means that 300 families survive on the money that comes from IFFCO.

There are many such societies across India that are surviving because of the manner in which Awasthi has managed and expanded IFFCO.

'He is a man with the golden touch,' said Simachal Padhi, a director from Odisha.

Awasthi is also very punctilious about meeting all legal obligations. Prem Chand Munshi, a director from Bihar, said, 'Can you name one company in the country, whether in the public or private or cooperative sectors, where the audited balance sheet is approved by the board and the dividend distributed to the shareholders within sixty days?'

IFFCO does it. The entire operation is transparent, open and IT based, leaving no scope for any irregularities.

But what sets Awasthi apart from other CEOs is his human touch. Unlike the managing directors of other companies who attend AGMs, deliver their speeches and leave, he makes it a point to mingle with the delegates.

Old-timers in IFFCO say he is the first managing director of the company to do so. He knows most delegates by name, and this helps him retain a direct line of contact with the real owners of the company—the farmers of India.

Mangi Lal Danga, a director from Rajasthan, adds that 'IFFCO has been in the service of farmers through cooperative societies, which are constituted by the farmers. Awasthi's contribution is that IFFCO now enjoys the complete trust of farmers.'

To help them, Awasthi clamped down on black marketing of fertilizers after taking over as IFFCO's managing director. 'If IFFCO fertilizers are available, then no trader can do black marketing. If they are not, then they sell at whatever prices they want,' informs Danga.

Helping start-ups

Then, Awasthi unveiled the next step of his vision for helping farmers—a start-up fund. He said: 'Why don't we fund some start-ups? In what ways can we fund start-ups? One way is to give them money.' But money is not in short supply for good projects.

When the IFFCO team spoke to entrepreneurs, they found that the entrepreneurs had good projects, good ideas and good execution models but they lacked the ability to reach out to farmers. That's when IFFCO thought it could provide its own reach to farmers to support start-ups in return for equity or money.

'We called a few entrepreneurs. They all said: yes, this makes a lot of sense to us. So that was one activity we got into,' said Manish Gupta.

'The IFFCO eBazar was the precursor of the ICDP,' said Yogendra Kumar.

Awasthi led the campaign from the front.

The golden jubilee was one of the greatest milestones in the history of IFFCO. Awasthi travelled across the country to meet farmers and co-operators to find out first-hand what they wanted in the future. During his travels, he found there was a big gap in their digital knowledge and information.

The golden jubilee celebrations thus led to the creation of a new digital platform that brought together various co-operators and farmers from the entire country with different mindsets and languages.

This, in turn, led to the creation of ICDP. Further, when IFFCO grew, it found that this could be converted into a big revenue generating model. Later, that model morphed into IFFCO eBazar, which provides things required by farmers at their doorstep without charging any delivery costs.

It was another feather in Awasthi's cap.

Carnival-like atmosphere at AGMs

IFFCO AGMs have gained a reputation of being gala events. The AGM was organized in the NCUI premises. It's an expansive campus with a big auditorium and a very large open field. More than 2,000 people attended the function. Breakfast was served at 8.00 a.m. to about 1,500 guests.

A beaming Awasthi arrived at 10.00 a.m. As he mingled with the delegates, he was almost mobbed by the crowd, which wanted selfies and photographs with him. He was barely able to walk a few steps when a new group surrounded him, eager to get photographed with him. It took him two hours to cover a distance of a few hundred metres.

People finally settled into the auditorium. The chairman was escorted to the dais, followed by Awasthi and other board members. The AGM opened with the chairman's speech. He gave an account of the previous year's performance and spelt out the future plans. The joint managing director then read out the agenda.

It was Awasthi's turn to speak. The auditorium reverberated with applause as he walked to the mike. He delivered a brief speech and then asked the delegates if they had any misgivings about the agenda. They all shouted 'no' in unison. He thanked them and settled down in his chair.

It was then the turn of the delegates to give their suggestions. Men and women in colourful attire came forward to speak.

Meanwhile, lunch was announced, and the gift counters opened. People began to stream out of the auditorium.

Ramachandran is a young delegate from Coimbatore. 'I am also a director on the board of IKST,' he said, adding that he had come to see Awasthi. 'He is not just popular. He is revered like a messiah,' he said about the IFFCO managing director.

IFFCO bags awards at FAI seminar

The FAI annual seminar in 2017 was held at Pullman Hotel in New Delhi's Aerocity. The function was inaugurated by the Minister of Chemicals and Fertilizers, Ananth Kumar. The chairman of FAI, K.S. Raju, who is also the chairman of Nagarjuna Fertilizers and Chemicals Limited, gave a candid account of the plight of the fertilizer industry in the country.

After the speeches, the awards were announced. IFFCO won the maximum number of awards. Each time IFFCO's name was announced, the auditorium reverberated with applause from IFFCO executives.

The award function concluded with the announcement of two U.S. Awasthi IFFCO Awards, one for Lifetime Achievement in the Fertilizer Sector, and the other for Lifetime Achievement in the Field of Agriculture.

That was the year the awards were instituted. They are now given annually at the FAI seminar. Each award is presented with a gold medallion, a citation and a cheque for ₹25 lakh. That year, Pratap Narayan and R.S. Paroda were the two awardees.

Pratap Narayan is a former bureaucrat who came to the Department of Fertilizers on deputation, way back in 1978, and thereafter remained involved with the fertilizer industry. After retiring from the government, he became the director general of FAI and held that position for seventeen years. He is credited with integrating India with the world fertilizer fraternity. Awasthi became president of IFA during Narayan's tenure at FAI.

R.S. Paroda is a well-known agricultural scientist who is credited with spearheading and modernizing the system of agricultural research in the country. He is the main architect of the National Gene Bank, which is the second largest in the world. He has received several national and international awards and recognitions, including the Padma Bhushan in 1998 and the Norman Borlaug Award in 2006.

Jordan investment finalized in three days

Mohammad Thneibat, the ex-deputy prime minister of Jordan, attended the next FAI seminar the following year. He is also the chairman of the Jordan India Fertiliser Company and the Jordan Phosphate Mines Company (JPMC), IFFCO's JVs in Jordan.

He met Awasthi for the first time in 2016. He said, 'I was on an official visit to India. He invited me to a dinner where a group of people came to discuss issues pertaining to IFFCO, JPMC, rock phosphate and related issues. After that, he accompanied me to three of his plants—in Kalol, Kandla and Paradeep. I also attended IFFCO's golden jubilee celebrations in Ahmedabad. So, I had many opportunities to meet him and spend time with him,' he said about the IFFCO managing director.

He quotes an Arabian proverb—one can't know a person till one has travelled with him and had monetary dealings with him. 'I consider myself to be one of the people from outside India who knows Awasthi very well. We travelled together. We dealt with each other in formal business. We talked a lot about our mutual interests,' he said.

Thneibat is quite unabashedly an Awasthi admirer. 'I find Awasthi a great man. He is honest, he lives up to his word and he is a good decision-maker. Once he is convinced of an idea, he does not hesitate to implement that immediately. I consider myself a good decision-maker and often have a very aggressive approach towards business, but I have always found my friend Awasthi far ahead of me,' he said.

Six months prior to that, IFFCO and IPL had together bought some shares in JPMC. They now own 37 per cent of the company. 'We talked a lot about this issue and when I told him this would be a very promising investment, he did not hesitate. He just took my word for it and made the deal. It did not take much time,' said the Deputy Prime Minister of Jordan.

'It took three days to seal the deal that involved an investment of $120 million,' informs Manish Gupta.

A dreamer

Awasthi likes to call himself a dreamer. He said, 'I keep dreaming about what might happen next. I am always thinking about alternative scenarios. My style of management is poetic.'

It was these dreams that led IFFCO into the power sector in Chhattisgarh. Many mega power plants were then in the pipeline. They were all coal based as gas prices were very high. There was an acute shortage of power in the country. The government was going to purchase power from these projects at very high prices.

Awasthi wanted to set up a coal-based power plant, produce power at the cheapest possible cost, and make a part of that power available to farmers at a discounted rate. IFFCO commissioned a study and realized it could set up a power plant 10 kilometres from the Tarapur coal block in Chhattisgarh.

It signed an MOU with the state government for a company in which it would hold 76 per cent. The remaining 24 per cent was to be held by the Chhattisgarh government.

But as the project progressed, several hurdles cropped up. The state government wanted IFFCO to contribute its share of equity in the company. Awasthi refused. 'This is a commercial enterprise that must follow commercial ethics. You have to contribute your equity,' he told the state government.

The government started dilly-dallying. Then the project faced environmental hurdles. Awasthi went to meet Jairam Ramesh, who was then Minister of Environment and Forests, and made a presentation to him. He was so impressed that he gave Awasthi a six-page-long favourable order.

But the Supreme Court cancelled all the coal block allocations. That was the end of IFFCO's tryst with the power sector.

'I don't think there was any major expenditure other than the payment of ₹66 crore for the mining lease,' said Awasthi.

IFFCO also invested in the National Commodity & Derivatives Exchange Limited (NCDEX). 'NCDEX is a very important initiative for farmers in the country. After IFFCO-Tokio, we wanted to diversify into some more financial services where we could provide help to farmers.

We had considered the option of banking, but decided that it was not suitable for us then,' said Awasthi, explaining the reasoning behind his expansion plans.

It was around this time that two national commodity exchanges were established—the Multi Commodity Exchange of India Ltd (MCX) and NCDEX. IFFCO chose NCDEX because it had more credible promoters, like the National Bank for Agriculture and Rural Development, the National Stock Exchange, LIC, ICICI Bank and some nationalized banks. Also, unlike MCX where emphasis was more on bullions and other such items, NCDEX predominantly dealt in agri-commodities. Rakesh Kapur is a member of the board of directors at NCDEX.

Farmers remain at the core of IFFCO's vision

'Farmers are the unmistakable focus of all our endeavours,' said Yogendra Kumar. 'IFFCO's hallmark is its connection with farmers at the grassroots level. They are our owners and consumers. In 2018, Fortune India listed IFFCO as the 43rd largest company in India. We are the only cooperative in this list.'

'Through all these achievements, Dr Awasthi never lost sight of India's farmers and its villages. After every brief interlude, he launched a major programme for farmers,' he said.

Awasthi launched IFFDC as soon as he took over as managing director. It is now a multi-state cooperative society engaged in major projects to bring the rural poor into the economic mainstream. And every few years since then, he has come out with new initiatives that focus on farmers.

In doing so, Awasthi, the dreamer, has been making life easier for India's farmers.

EIGHT

GOING BIG WITH NANO

We live in the age of disruptive technologies. How quickly we adapt to them defines our place in the world order. Just as the Industrial Revolution turned horses and elephants from being means of transport to showpieces, so also technologies that are in use today will be obsolete tomorrow, and what looks technologically unattainable now will be commonplace in the future.

Awasthi has always believed that society should be technologically agile. If we have to save our planet, then we will have to replace the present technological paradigm, he said, adding that fertilizers, which are at the core of IFFCO's existence, will also be replaced.

'We will have nano-fertilizers. We will have alternative forms of nutrient management. We have, therefore, constituted a team that is conducting cutting-edge research on this,' he adds.

Awasthi had just returned from a short vacation in the US in the second half of 2017 when he told some members of his team that he was seriously thinking of launching nano-fertilizers.

'He had been worried about the deleterious effects of conventional chemical fertilizers and had been calling upon the fertilizer fraternity on all national and international platforms to find an alternative to them,' said Yogendra Kumar. 'Our foray into water soluble fertilizers, biofertilizers, organic fertilizers, plant growth promoters, etc., were steps in this direction. So as soon as he learnt about the possibility of nano-fertilizers, he started working on them in right earnest.'

Investing in nano-technology

Awasthi had been talking about nano-technology in fertilizers for a long time, but he became serious about it when he read in a journal that research on nano-fertilizers had reached a critical stage.

He asked his team to look for the most reputed scientist in the country on nano-fertilizers. After a brief search, the team zeroed in on Dr J.C. Tarafdar and recruited him and his team. In June 2018, the IFFCO Tarafdar Nano Lab was set up at the company's mother plant in Kalol.

The Tarafdar team developed many biological nano-fertilizers—like nano-nitrogen, nano-zinc and nano-phosphorous. However, when field trials were carried out, they could not produce the desired results.

In June 2019, the IFFCO Tarafdar Nano Lab was discontinued. All this while, IFFCO had been in touch with a young scientist, Dr Ramesh Raliya, who had completed his PhD under Dr Tarafdar. He was working on nano-fertilizers at Washington University in St. Louis.

A new beginning

In 2019, IFFCO Joint Managing Director Rakesh Kapur and Kumar went to St Louis to attend a seminar. Dr Raliya, who is in his early thirties, was one of the speakers at that seminar.

'We met him after the seminar. Since we had been in touch over phone and WhatsApp, we could cut to the chase right away,' said Kumar. 'He told us that he had sent samples of his nano-fertilizers to his home state Rajasthan and that the farmers there were using them.'

This sounded very promising. He took Kapur and Kumar to see his laboratory, which was very impressive. Then, he took them to see his field trials with soyabean and corn about one hundred kilometres away.

Both Kapur and Kumar got the feeling that Dr Raliya could perhaps lead them to their holy grail. They asked if he could visit India to meet Awasthi. By a happy coincidence, he had been planning to visit India the following month.

He replied in the affirmative.

It was a very fruitful meeting: Awasthi made him an offer, asking him to join IFFCO. He told him that IFFCO would meet all his expectations and provide all the facilities he needed to set up a world-class research centre in India. It had always been IFFCO's endeavour to make the world's best technology available to the farmers of the country, he added.

'If that is really so, then I would definitely like to work with IFFCO,' Dr Raliya responded.

'You can decide now, or you can decide later. I will tell you in one sentence that whatever you want, I will make available to you in IFFCO. Do your research and work for the farmers. If you want to work in India, then there is no other organization here like IFFCO. It will provide you with an open platform. You do whatever you want to do. We will provide you with all the support,' Awasthi reiterated.

These words gave the young scientist the confidence to consider giving up a bright and financially rewarding future in the US and returning to India. 'If I join, what will be the terms and conditions?' he asked Awasthi.

'I will provide you with all the support. The rest you discuss with Yogendra Kumar, R.P. Singh and Rakesh Kapur. You finalize your terms with them,' Awasthi told him.

He joined the newly established IFFCO Nano Biotechnology Research Center soon thereafter. The young scientist was ready with the first sample of nano-zinc by the end of his first month at IFFCO. Soon, he also developed nano-nitrogen (urea) and nano-copper.

Ushering in a revolution

IFFCO filed for the patent of its nano-fertilizers in October, barely three months after the establishment of the research centre. Away from the lights, IFFCO was ushering in a global revolution that could herald a new era in plant management.

The next step was to conduct field trials and then apply to the government for approvals. As the trials were carried out on IFFCO's own farmlands in Kalol, the Department of Agriculture declined approval. 'These field trials are not sufficient. You have to conduct them on the lands of farmers, in agricultural research institutes, and in universities under the observation of scientists and then come to us with the results,' it said.

Awasthi said: 'Fine, we will launch nationwide field trials,' and set the date of 3 November 2019, IFFCO's fifty-second birth anniversary. By this time, Dr Raliya had set up a pilot plant, which was producing 6,000 bottles of nano-nitrogen, nano-zinc and nano-copper every day.

Awasthi made elaborate plans. He said that the trials of the three products would be launched simultaneously at 11,000 places around the country and that at least two farmers from each state would attend the inauguration in person.

A long and winding road

It was a humongous task and a massive logistics challenge—all the 11,000 locations had to be digitally mapped. If the chief guest or any other dignitary wanted to see the trial at any specific place in the country, it could be shown in real time from Kalol itself. As with all programmes where Awasthi was present, it was a mega function—nearly 2,000 farmers from Gujarat were present to witness the event.

'All set for the launch of IFFCO nano-technology-based products from our mother unit at Kalol by Sh. D.V. Sadananda Gowda-ji, Union Minister of Chemicals & Fertilizers, Sh. Mansukh L. Mandaviya-ji, Minister of State for Chemicals & Fertilizers, Sh. P.K. Rupala-ji, Minister of State for Agriculture,' Awasthi tweeted.

The dignitaries then went to see IFFCO's laboratory and other facilities. They were very impressed. Each of them was gifted a bottle each of nano-nitrogen, nano-zinc and nano-copper. Gowda said IFFCO's innovations would put an end to the use of conventional urea and create a pollution-free environment for drinking water, soil and air.

The field trials were done on ninety-four crops. Simultaneously, trials were also carried out at Krishi Vigyan Kendras. Then, field trials were carried out on forty-three crops in twenty leading agricultural universities and ICAR research institutes.

Awasthi was personally involved in this process. He asked for weekly reports on the progress of the trials and even went to meet the people in the field wherever necessary.

The results were very encouraging. There was an increase of 8 per cent in yields, the consumption of urea was reduced by half and, most importantly, the quality of yields was significantly better. These trials also dispelled the fear that nano-fertilizers might harm crops and the environment.

The Tamil Nadu Agricultural University had lots of ongoing nano-projects. It tested IFFCO's new products for toxicity and found that they had no effect on soil microbes or elements. The new fertilizers were found to be absolutely non-toxic.

The Organization for Economic Cooperation and Development has guidelines that many developed countries follow. The new products were found to be compliant with them.

On 7 July 2020, the Department of Biotechnology issued its guidelines for nano-products. The three products, nano-nitrogen, nano-zinc and nano-copper, were tested according to those guidelines. They passed all the tests.

Then, IFFCO applied to the Department of Agriculture to include them in the Fertilizer Control Order (FCO) as fertilizers cannot be sold in the market unless they are listed in the FCO. The Department of Agriculture formed a committee called Central Fertilizer Committee (CFC) to evaluate the applications.

The Agriculture Commissioner of the Government of India chaired the CFC. The members asked lots of questions and gave their recommendation only after all these were satisfactorily answered.

All the CFC members agreed that these three products should be registered on the basis of the results obtained by the agricultural universities and ICAR institutes, but the chairman did not agree.

'It's not clear if the tests have been done according to the guidelines of the Department of Biotechnology. The three products are very promising on the basis of their efficacy, but we cannot recommend their registration unless the Department of Biotechnology does the tests and confirms that they conform to its guidelines,' the chairman of CFC said.

The IFFCO products had already been tested according to the Department of Biotechnology guidelines. The material it had submitted to CFC ran into tens of thousands of pages. It had the results of all sorts of toxicity tests—including their impact on bees, fishes, the embryos of fishes, on chicken and on all categories of living organisms.

Nevertheless, the scientists of the Department of Biotechnology carried out all the tests once again. Many rounds of meetings were held; there were long sessions of questions and answers. Finally, they said these products were fine. But CFC approved only nano-nitrogen in the form of nano-urea (liquid). It withheld approval for nano-zinc and nano-copper.

The director of the Indian Institute of Toxicology Research in Lucknow, Dr S.K. Barik, had especially been invited to the CFC. He said zinc and copper have long-term toxicity problems, so they cannot be approved without long-term trials. On the basis of his comment, the approval for nano-zinc and nano-copper was withheld. Awasthi said their trials must not stop. More universities have joined the trials.

Awasthi recalls, 'We had a discussion with Dr Barik and told him that we had completed two years of trials. He said: "You continue with your trials for one more year; we will then test and approve your products." So, IFFCO is very hopeful that it will be able to launch nano-zinc and nano-copper in the near future.'

In February 2021, the Government of India approved the use of IFFCO nano-urea (liquid) and included it in the FCO. On 31 May 2021, at IFFCO's fiftieth AGM, Awasthi announced the commercial production and sale of IFFCO nano-urea (liquid). 'We are introducing the first nano-urea produced by IFFCO for farmers across the world,' said Awasthi.

The efficiency of this nano-urea was improved in collaboration with Nano Biotechnology Research Center and a south-based scientific organization. This product is longer lasting and has received an excellent response on the ground. The patent has been also filed, and Awasthi's name has appeared there too.

The nano-urea is manufactured in a state-of-the-art facility with a capacity to produce 1.5 lakh bottles per day. The entire process is automated. No human hand touches the product. The first point of human contact is when the boxes containing nano-urea bottles have to be loaded on to trucks.

On account of combined efforts of the Nano Bio Research Centre and Nano Ventions led by Dr Lakshmanan, presently available IFFCO nano-urea (liquid) is most stable and has superior qualities.

The journey of developing nano-fertilizers has been full of ups and downs. During tough times, he boosted the morale of his team. 'We lost some senior scientists in between, but our efforts continued,' says Awasthi. He always has a contingency plan and thus manages with ease.

Apart from the Chairman and the Board of IFFCO, he also expresses his gratitude to Dr Mansukh Mandaviya, Minister of Health and Family

Welfare and Minister of Chemicals and Fertilizers, for his strong support for nano-fertilizers.

How it works

Nano-urea addresses the problems that ordinary urea brings in its wake. Plants absorb almost 30 per cent of the urea that is applied as fertilizer. The remaining 70 per cent urea harms the environment in many ways. For example, the urea travels into the air as nitrous oxide (NO_x), which is a greenhouse gas that causes global warming and climate change. There is emission of ammonia, which increases NO_x in the atmosphere and pollutes the air. The unused urea in the soil affects its pH value and prevents plants from absorbing other nutrients.

It also pollutes water—the urea in the field mixes with water and flows into canals and underground water sources and increases the number of nitrates in the water. Leaching also takes place, which further contaminates the underground water.

'Nano-urea has nearly 86 per cent use efficiency. In terms of volumes, 500 ml of nano-urea has the same potency as a 45 kg bag of regular urea. Ordinary urea contains 46 per cent nitrogen. We usually apply two bags of urea in an acre of land. That means 41 kg of nitrogen gets into the soil. Of this, only 30–40 per cent is absorbed by plants; so, approximately16–28 kg of nitrogen is left over in an acre of land,' explains Dr Raliya.

'A 500 ml bottle of nano-urea has 20 gm nitrogen. If we apply two bottles of nano-urea in an acre of land, and assuming that plants absorb 86 per cent nitrogen, then the leftover nitrogen in an acre of land is barely 5–6 gm, which is negligible. Thus, nano-urea almost entirely eliminates the harmful effects of ordinary urea,' he adds.

Keeping it affordable

When the product was almost ready, Awasthi asked his scientist, 'What, according to you, should be the price of the nano-fertilizer you have developed?'

'Sir, in the US, it will cost thousands of dollars.'

When Awasthi saw the cost of production, he said, 'Keep the price at ₹240 and finally he made it ₹225.' A bottle contains 500 ml. Awasthi said the quantity should never be less than 500 ml.

'Now, a 500 ml bottle of nano-urea costs about ₹225, whereas a 45 kg bag of ordinary urea costs ₹268, with a government subsidy of around ₹2,000. So, the real cost of the bag is ₹2,268. The subsidy on a bag of ordinary DAP is ₹2,500. The total subsidy on all fertilizers in our country is around ₹1.5 lakh crore every year,' said Kumar.

India can, thus, save a massive amount of money every year if the entire country switches to nano-fertilizers. 'We will have more production, the quality of produce will be better, without any harm to our soil, water, or air. That's why nano-fertilizers are being called a revolution. They herald the beginning of a new era in plant nutrient management,' said Kumar.

In his reply to a question in Parliament on 13 December 2022, Minister of Agriculture and Farmers' Welfare Narendra Singh Tomar said: 'ICAR in association with IFFCO, has agronomically evaluated IFFCO nano-urea in Rabi and Kharif crops. Nano-urea will lead to savings for farmers. Two rounds of sprays of nano-urea along with recommended basal dose of nitrogen have led to increased yields of 3–8 per cent in various cops and 25–30 per cent savings in urea.'

The other advantage of nano-fertilizers lies in its storage and transportation. Let us do the maths: a 500 ml bottle of nano-urea replaces a 45 kg bag of urea. The total consumption of fertilizers in the country is around 61.4 million tonnes per year. That means 61.4 million tonnes of ordinary fertilizers can be replaced by nano-fertilizers.

'Imagine the amount of money the country can save in terms of transportation and storage from the point of production to the point of consumption if ordinary fertilizers are converted into nano-fertilizers,' said Kumar.

Union Home Minister Amit Shah who also holds the Cooperation portfolio, lauded IFFCO and its managing director while laying the foundation stone of the ₹450 crore nano-urea plant in Deoghar, Jharkhand, on 4 February 2023. 'First of all, in the whole world, IFFCO made nano-urea, it is a matter of pride for India. I have been in contact with Awasthi for the last four years and his hard work of four to five years has paid off. After a lot of hard work, it has been brought to the end. Awasthi-ji has worked very hard behind this project, I know,' he said.

Addressing the event, Shah added that liquid urea is being exported to about five countries. He said the liquid urea made by IFFCO would not only help Indian farmers but also those all over the world.

Union Minister of Chemicals and Fertilizers Mansukh Mandaviya tweeted: 'After nano-urea, the government has now given approval to nano DAP as well... This is one more achievement towards achieving self-sufficiency in fertilizers.'

A boon for the agricultural sector

The initial response of farmers to the launch of nano-fertilizers has been very positive and, for IFFCO, very encouraging. Farmers across India, from Karnataka and Andhra Pradesh in the south to Uttar Pradesh, Jammu and Kashmir, Punjab, Haryana and Himachal Pradesh in the north, to Assam, Bihar, West Bengal and Odisha in the east to Maharashtra and Gujarat in the west, have reported very good results from using this new type of soil nutrient.

They have reported 6 per cent to 35 per cent higher yields and significantly higher incomes after experimenting with nano-fertilizers on small portions of their agricultural land. Seeing them, other farmers in their villages, who may have been wary of using a new product in place of tried-and-tested ones, are now switching to nano-fertilizers.

For example, Chanene Govada, a farmer in Chananahalli village near Bengaluru, used nano-urea on his 15 acre farm and got 35 per cent higher output of maize, which increased his profits by ₹25,000 Seeing this, 30 other farmers in his village have also started using nano-urea.

Farmers' own technology

India still uses foreign technology to make urea. But nano-urea is a product of indigenous research. 'This is a technology that belongs to Indian farmers. IFFCO is a society of farmers, so it is the technology *of* the farmers of this country. Farmers are making fertilizers for themselves with their own technology,' said Awasthi.

IFFCO has filed many patents in India and abroad. 'This is one of the most remarkable things we have done. We have also developed eight different products that will be commercialized in the near future,' informs Kumar.

IFFCO has developed a nano-hand sanitizer, nano-zinc, nano-copper, nano-boron, nano-sulphur and nano-DAP. 'We are going to develop a multi-nutrient mixture and organic nano-fertilizers. We have another product, called "Sagarika." We will use Sagarika to develop some nano-formulations,' he adds.

Awasthi is planning to convert all of IFFCO's agricultural inputs into nano-based ones. 'This is what our scientists also say. We have developed nano-sulphur and nano-boron as well. Their field trials are taking place across the country. There are many more products in the pipeline that our scientists are researching on,' said the marketing director of IFFCO.

The way forward

IFFCO nano-fertilizers are a step in the direction of self-reliance in terms of Atmanirbhar Bharat and Atmanirbhar Krishi. Widespread adoption of nano-urea and other nano-fertilizers will lead to an increase in farmers' profitability and in addressing India's sustainable development goals. IFFCO is bringing an extensive range of nano-fertilizers—nano-DAP, nano-NPK, nano-zinc, nano-copper, nano-boron, nano-sulphur, etc.—for eco-friendly, sustainable agriculture

The success of nano-urea (liquid) whetted Awasthi's appetite for further advances in the field of nano fertilizers. At his urging and under his guidance IFFCO scientists developed nano-DAP, which can address the phosphorous nutrition needs of crops better than traditional phosphatic fertilizers, which suffer from low efficiency of less than 20 per cent, not to speak of a huge drainage of resources and the spread of pollution to soil, air and water. 'I thought deeply about this issue, discussed it with IFFCO's scientists and directed them to go look for alternatives and also go for maximum nutrient loading in our nano-DAP. We could utilize the lessons learnt during our nano-urea journey. We reached out to Dr A. Lakshamanan of Nano Ventions Private Limited (NVPL), Coimbatore, to achieve maximum clear nano-clusters formation,' said Awasthi.

The product performed well in field efficacy trials conducted on different crops in different agroclimatic regions across the country both as seed/seedling treatment and as foliar application.

IFFCO's nano-DAP provides benefit to crops equivalent or more than that provided by a bag of conventional DAP. It also fulfils all the bio-efficacy, bio-safety and bio-toxicity norms as per industry standards and the Department of Biotechnology's guidelines. It has been estimated that the use of nano-DAP will increase crop yields by 6–7 per cent.

'We submitted the nano-DAP results to the Ministry of Agriculture & Farmers Welfare, Government of India, on 22 March 2022. After successive meetings of the CFC, nano-DAP was included in the FCO on 2 March 2023,' said a delighted Awasthi.

Commercial production of nano-DAP began at IFFCO-NVPL, Coimbatore. Production will commence at IFFCO-Kalol units in the near future. In due course, other IFFCO units at Paradeep and Kandla will also start producing this product. By 2024–2025, IFFCO plans to produce 17 crore to 22 crore bottles of nano-DAP.

'Work on nano-NPK (8-8-8), nano-sulphur, nano-zinc and nano-copper is also at advanced stages and my vision is that IFFCO will soon make complete crop nutrition solutions through nano-fertilizers available to farmers,' adds the IFFCO managing director.

Lauding the development, Prime Minister Modi tweeted on 3 March 2023: 'This is a part of our various efforts to bring a long-term difference to the lives of our farmers.'

The future of nano-technology

A revolution comes when there are dramatic shifts in certain practices—shifts away from the way things have been done. 'They represent a sudden quantum jump,' said a senior scientist at IFFCO. He gives the example of the Green Revolution; India was importing food earlier, now India exports food.

He said, 'Nano-technology will be the next revolution. It will help India in multiple ways. Today, we are working on fertilizers and agrochemicals, but tomorrow it may be used in other sectors, such as food packaging, nutraceuticals, pharmaceuticals, sensors, defence technologies, the space sector and many others. That means IFFCO will not remain confined to fertilizers or agriculture in the future.'

The young scientist is visibly proud of his creation. 'In the entire world, you won't find any single facility that can develop nano-materials at this large scale. Here, we are producing 1.5 lakh bottles per day. It has the ability to manufacture nano-materials with consistent quality. No other company in the world has done this so far. Other companies may be much larger or have a bigger footprint globally, but they will be hard pressed to match our all-round ability,' he said.

IFFCO has further commissioned the Aonla and Phulpur units of nano-urea (liquid) with a combined capacity of 12 crore bottles per year. Dr Mansukh Mandaviya, Minister of Health and Family Welfare and Minister of Chemical and Fertiliser inaugurated them on 12th February 2023.

Looking into the crystal ball

Awasthi foresees a future where IFFCO may contribute to the defence industry in India, work with the Indian Space Research Organisation (ISRO) and contribute to the development of medicines. ISRO, NASA, the European Space Agency and the Russian Space Agency are all working on growing plants in space.

'IFFCO has the capability to grow plants in space with smart nutrients,' said an IFFCO scientist. 'From sensor technologies to pharmaceuticals, medicines to defence—the sky is the limit for nano-technology. We can develop anything. Dr Awasthi is rock solid behind us. He never said no to ideas.'

What IFFCO scientists like most is that Awasthi never interferes with their work. 'He is an exceptional listener. He cultivates people, he shares his vision and supports his people. But he never interferes with your expertise. He has his own vision, but he values expert opinion,' he said.

The R&D unit, which Awasthi has established at Kalol, will, thus, contribute across sectors in the years to come. 'It may take two years or twenty, but down the line, people from different sectors will thank Dr Awasthi for establishing this unit,' predicts Kumar.

NINE

LEADER OF ALL, MASTER TO NONE

Awasthi is one of India's longest serving professional chief executives. First as CMD of PPCL, then as CMD of RCF, and finally, as managing director of IFFCO, he has occupied various corner offices for the last thirty-six years. In an environment where public sector chief executives went in and out of the revolving door every time political masters changed, he has had the distinction of serving as MD and CEO under nine prime ministers, from Rajiv Gandhi to Narendra Modi and under thirty-six ministers.

This is as much a testament to his ability as a manager as to his felicity in navigating the political cross-currents that executives manning the topmost echelons of India's corporate hierarchy invariably have to master.

From the very outset, Awasthi was seen to possess an X factor that distinguished him from his peers. He lived up to that early billing by becoming one of India's youngest public-sector CMDs at the age of forty-one.

Rakesh Kapur, joint managing director of IFFCO, who has worked with him for twenty-two years, said, 'I could see that among public sector chief executives, Dr Awasthi stood out distinctly as a much more knowledgeable, efficient and result-oriented person.' He was particularly impressed by his boss's ability to come up with innovative ideas to expedite whatever task was at hand and thus avoid delays in projects.

'He is an entrepreneur rather than a mere manager. If you look at his period in IFFCO's corner office, you will find that there has been continuous growth. Even in the worst conditions, our returns have been far better than those of others in the fertilizer industry,' said Kamal Verma*, Senior Executive Director, Finance, IFFCO, who had worked closely with him since 1993.

Since fertilizer prices are controlled by the government, the only way to increase profits is to reduce costs by expanding volumes. 'He doubled the capacities of our plants and lowered their costs of production through energy savings projects and other measures. Then, he diversified into various other businesses and reduced the dependence on fertilizers,' he informs.

As a result of his vision and far-sightedness, IFFCO has earned profits of ₹1,000 crore or more every year since 2010.

'I was in marketing then and sometimes went to meet him with the marketing director. My direct boss was supposed to have the best knowledge of marketing, but Dr Awasthi always had more data and better knowledge than him. He always gave us some solutions,' Verma remembers. This is in addition to Awasthi's mastery of project management and thorough knowledge of the technology that goes into IFFCO's plants.

Thorough professional

His peers consider him a thorough professional. P.S. Gahlaut, managing director of IPL, who is himself considered a legend of the fertilizer industry, said, 'There are many directors on our board who see IPL as a competitor and a rival. Their questioning, their behaviour, their attitude reflect that. But not Awasthi—when he comes to our board meetings, he stands for what is good for IPL.'

*He died in 2020.

This ability to keep his own interests separate from those of the organization he is serving has won Awasthi great admiration and contributed significantly to his success.

Gahlaut also respects the IFFCO managing director for his undiluted focus on the welfare of India's farmers. 'I have seen him as chairman of FAI and IFA. When there is a trade-off between companies and farmers, we tend to look after the interests of the company—after all, they provide our bread and butter [...] but in many such situations, Awasthi has said, "We will take the hit; let us protect the farmers."'

He has gone out of his way to safeguard the interests of farmers even at the cost of annoying his own executives and his colleagues in the industry. 'If the prices have come down internationally, he will be the first to pass them on to the farmers. We all think we will lower the prices when releasing fresh stocks and recover some losses in the meanwhile,' said Gahlaut, adding that Awasthi's commitment to the country's farmers is absolute.

Late Raj Kumar Tripathi, a nominated director on the board of IFFCO, concurs. 'There are many instances when IFFCO has borne the brunt of price hikes in the international market and supplied fertilizers to famers at regular prices,' he said.

'I got to know him well during IFFCO's golden jubilee celebrations. As a director, vice chairman, and now chairman, I can say that his work over the last 40 years has had an impact from the ground level to the international market,' said Dileep Sanghani, chairman of IFFCO, about Awasthi.

'IFFCO is a manufacturer of fertilizers; selling fertilizers is its core business. He achieves his business objectives, and farmers get fertilizers at fair prices,' adds Vijay Shankar Rai, director on the board of Kisan International Trading, and presently a co-opted director of IFFCO.

This trait of Awasthi's—of being able to see the big picture and to pursue the greatest common good—was clearly in evidence in his avatar as head of associations like FAI and IFA.

Gahlaut explains, 'You go to the government with a single position that the industry wants this relief. Now, someone will benefit by two hundred rupees, someone else by three hundred rupees and others still by only fifty rupees. Many people take a stand depending on how much it suits them. But in the interest of building a consensus, Awasthi would often say: "Okay, IFFCO will take a hit, but I don't mind because it is for the larger good of the industry." I have not seen that magnanimity in others.'

Earned everyone fortunes

As chief executive, Awasthi has displayed a special ability to take everyone along and tie the well-being of individual stakeholders to that of the organization.

'All our JVs are huge successes. They have made IFFCO the world's largest fertilizer cooperative. These have brought great prosperity to IFFCO employees. I think 40–50 per cent of them have earned fortunes they had never dreamt of,' said Ram Singh, former General Secretary of the IFFCO Officers' Association.

He lists the benefits: no fertilizer company in the country pays salaries as high as IFFCO or provides similar perquisites and privileges. 'Can you name one other organization in the country that gives scholarships to the children of its employees,' he asks rhetorically. If the child is a good student or good at sports or a good artist, IFFCO provides support to help hone his/her skills.

'He manages to weave everyone's interests together very successfully,' said Rai.

Ability to deal with people from all backgrounds

Awasthi's people management skills are very much in evidence in his dealings with IFFCO's board of directors. Unlike the private sector or even the public sector, IFFCO is a cooperative. It's board, therefore, reflects is ownership structure—and comprises mostly politicians and/or farmers' representatives from different parts of the country. Very often, they represent the grassroots of rural India.

These people know India as well as anyone else, but they are not corporate professionals. It is not always easy to convince such a diverse group of individuals to go along with a particular corporate strategy.

But Awasthi's ability to build consensus and carry the board along has ensured the smooth functioning of the organization for more than a quarter-century.

His skill at getting along with people from diverse backgrounds has enabled Awasthi to build a great team of managers at IFFCO and its subsidiaries. He has this knack of being able to identify talented individuals whom he then grooms for larger roles in the organization.

'He has built a great team at IFFCO. I have always seen competent people around him. He is very good at delegation—if you don't delegate you can never expand, you can never be successful. After all, no individual can build a company. So having a competent team and providing good leadership are essential ingredients of success. He has demonstrated that in ample measure,' said H.S. Bawa, former vice chairman of Zuari Agro Chemicals, and a friend of Awasthi's.

Breaking the inertia: Regular Promotions

Awasthi recognized early that IFFCO's real strength lay in its managers and workers, and he made every effort to ensure that everyone on its rolls felt a sense of ownership towards the organization.

Soon after taking over as managing director in 1993, he found that career stagnation was impacting the morale of the organization. Executives had to wait for six to seven years for a promotion from one grade to the next. He constituted a high-powered committee to find a way of easing this problem.

The Recruitments and Promotions guidelines came in 1994. Stagnation was taken care of, and a mechanism was introduced to automatically upgrade executives to the next grade on completion of a certain number of years of service.

Awasthi said, 'We have to create more and more avenues for diverting these people to newer assignments and responsibilities. If we create many more organizations, then they can move laterally to those, and more and more opportunities will be created.' His philosophy was to create a situation in which the leaders would be forced to perform. He set a target for promoting a certain number of executives to general managers, and a certain number to executive directors and so on.

IFFCO would meet the additional expenditure on account of these promotions by expanding its activities, by diversifying into new areas and by generating more and more revenues.

The general body meeting of the union and officers was organized in Phulpur. The association and union said the plan was not workable and should be thrown into the dustbin.

'It was a novelty because earlier, promotions were entirely based on vacancies. But we did not understand his ideas and opposed the recommendations of the committee. Back then, we apprehended that the organization would grow heavy at the top, which is not a good structure,' admits Ram Singh with a wry smile.

Awasthi said, 'Fine,' and left the meeting.

He walked through the middle of the crowd, but nobody had the guts to stop him or say anything. After a year, the officers' association and union had to accept that it had been wrong to reject the new guidelines and requested that he implement the recommendations of the committee.

'It was a very imaginative and ambitious plan, which has worked very well for us. We now have promotions every four to five years,' said Ram Singh.

Accessible to all

In line with Awasthi's management philosophy, IFFCO has a very transparent HR architecture—every level has clearly defined roles and responsibilities as well as perquisites and privileges. All these are clearly mentioned in an HR handbook, called the 'Induction Manual'. Rekha Mishra, a young woman executive in IFFCO's HR department, said, 'One person from each plant was part of the team that designed the manual. I was one of the members of the team.'

The head of IFFCO's public relations department presented this manual at a conference on mass communication in Delhi and it won an award. Everyone praised the PR team and the team leaders. When the HR team got to know of this, it asked its team leader why it had been ignored. The team leader escalated this to the Director, HR, at head office, who informed Awasthi about it.

He immediately called them for a cup of tea with him at the head office. 'Catch the next flight and come to the head office,' a message from the Managing Director's Secretariat said.

Awasthi met the team very warmly. 'You have done a fabulous job. Keep up your good work. We have very high expectations from the young generation,' he told them.

He had recently met Prime Minister Modi. He told the team about the meeting and praised the contribution of the female workforce in IFFCO. 'He acknowledges the good work of people—the person could be a senior officer or a junior employee. He is accessible to all,' said the lady executive.

It is this affability that endears him to everyone in IFFCO and reinforces the sense of belonging that pervades the organization.

Maintains good relations with workers

Harish Rawat, president of the Officers' Association of Aonla and founder president of the workers' union at the plant, said, 'I have seen many managing directors since I joined IFFCO. None of them had good relations with the unions and the associations. They did not have any contact with the common people. When Awasthi came, he began to involve everyone in the decision-making process.'

This instilled a sense of participation throughout the organization. When he bought the Paradeep plant, he made it a point to call the unions and associations and informed them about the development.

'He never imposes his decisions. He takes the lead, of course, but he consults everyone. That's why all his decisions have the strength of collective wisdom and mostly result in successful outcomes,' adds Rawat.

Awasthi takes pains to maintain excellent relations between the management and the workforce. There has been no strike in IFFCO for the last twenty-five years. There are workers' unions and officers' associations in all the five plants. Altogether there are six unions and six associations, and Awasthi's adroit handling of IFFCO's massive and growing workforce has ensured complete labour harmony.

R.P. Singh, Head of HR and Legal at IFFCO, said, 'Awasthi has earned a reputation for himself. The workers know the union leaders will not be able to get them something that is beyond reach. They also know the management will give it the maximum it can give. Awasthi does not like to bargain. When the unions and associations ask him for something, he said: "This is what is left in the reserve. You decide how much you should get."'

It is a measure of the goodwill that Awasthi enjoys with the unions that they agreed to a ten-year wage agreement instead of the usual practice of signing a wage accord for five years.

Prior to 2004, IFFCO was more or less like a public sector company. So, it was largely guided by public sector pay scales. After the repatriation of government equity, the next wage negotiation was to be effective from January 2007. Negotiations commenced in public sector companies, but nothing had been finalized. This meant that there was no benchmark available. IFFCO's senior executives advised Awasthi to wait for other companies to arrive at an agreement that could become the benchmark for the industry.

'Why should we wait for others? Why can't we take the lead and set the benchmark for others? Let's discuss and decide what we can afford on the basis of our own independent standing, our own business prospects and profitability,' Awasthi said.

His message was simple—you know the organization, you know its limitations, you know its strengths, and you have to keep in mind its challenges and prospects. 'On that basis, we should give the best that we can give,' he said.

It was a tall order because it is easier to negotiate when there is a benchmark. When there are none, unions tend to ask for the moon. They fear that if the other companies offer their workers better deals, they will have nothing to show their people.

Not surprisingly, the talks ended in a deadlock. Awasthi had to arbitrate between his executives and his workers. He told them, 'We are a cooperative society where there is no entrepreneur or businessman who has a motive for profit. Our profits are ploughed back into the organization or shared with our shareholders, who are farmers, or distributed among employees. So, we have to see that the organization can sustain, and that whatever money it makes is equitably distributed among the employees, the shareholders and the organization.'

Awasthi, who enjoys their trust, assured the unions that he would renegotiate the contract if any other company offered its workers a better deal than IFFCO. Awasthi's ability to distil a complex problem and explain its solution in simple layman's terms convinced the workers to sign a ten-year deal.

'Finally, we had a good settlement that became a benchmark for other fertilizer companies,' informs R.P. Singh.

Made PF, ESI compulsory for contractors' workers

In 1998, Awasthi was on a visit to the Phulpur plant. As he was walking around the plant, a daily wage earner fell at his feet and cried, 'Sir, we get very meagre wages and we do not have the security of provident fund (PF).'

That very evening, he made PF and the Employees' State Insurance Scheme compulsory for the workers employed by IFFCO contractors. 'Now, it will be a condition for awarding work to contractors,' he said. He also raised the wages by a certain percentage.

'Imagine the situation—wages of workers were revised, and their terms of employment changed in a running contract. The whole system was turned upside down. Things got very complicated for the contractors, but they had to implement the new wage structure,' said Jitendra Tiwari, president of the IFFCO Officers' Association at the head office.

Everyone in IFFCO is satisfied

Explaining his connect with common people, Awasthi said he has never believed that he is the boss of the company. 'We all are one and the same. Segregating people into categories causes separation between people. I am grateful to God that since childhood I have never considered anyone bigger or smaller than me.'

He can often turn philosophical and wistful. 'Life is full of ups and downs,' he said. 'Tides are natural to the ocean. They go up and come down. But the ocean remains intact.' He has drawn a lesson from that.

'This "I" is the ego that brings all the difficulties in your life and in your work. I still meet my childhood friends when I visit my village and

I also interact with heads of states. I find no difference between the two. I have my own ways of meeting them,' he said.

Visitors often say they get positive vibrations when they visit the IFFCO office. 'Everyone in IFFCO is satisfied. You will rarely find anyone with a sad face here. People are happily engaged in their work. Even the gossips are well-wishers of IFFCO and loyal,' said Kamal Verma.

People remain part of the IFFCO family even after retirement

IFFCO functions are usually spectacular showpiece events. They are also well attended by former IFFCO executives, who are given respect commensurate with their ranks at the time of their retirement and treated equitably. Former directors sit with the directors. Former chairmen are given seats among the VVIPs. If they are not alive, their wives receive the same treatment.

Then, there is a tradition of naming IFFCO's townships and buildings after its former chairmen and managing directors. IFFCO has named it's Kandla township as Uday Nagar after Uday Bhan Singh, who was the founding Chairman of IFFCO. Similarly, IFFCO has Paul Pothen Nagar at Aonla, a Surinder Jakhar Nagar at Paradeep, an L.R. Talwar Bhavan at Kandla and a B.S. Nakai Bhavan at Chandigarh and many others.

The township at the mother plant in Kalol has a special story attached to it. It is named after Kasturi Rangan, who was a Technical Advisor in the Department of Fertilizers when IFFCO was formed in 1967. Those were the days of Licence Raj. Kasturi Rangan had played a very important role in getting the licence allotted to IFFCO. The township is a tribute to his memory.

As usual, Awasthi has a very earthy reason for institutionalizing this value system in IFFCO. 'We have always tried to stay connected to our roots. Roots are very important; they give us life. If our roots are weak, if we forget about our history or forget about our culture, we can never grow beyond a level, after which we will fall. If the organization's roots are strong, if the foundation is sturdy, then we can go on expanding,' he explains.

Awasthi has inculcated a culture in IFFCO where employees remain connected even after retiring from the organization. 'So many employees retire every year. But this culture of treating everyone as part of the family is unique. I don't know how things are in other organizations, but such close bonding is not common in the corporate world. Regardless of whether a person is still working or has retired, he/she gets the same respect and the same kind of treatment from the company,' said M.K. Tandon, the first Finance Director Awasthi had appointed.

Tandon has especially fond memories. He retired from IFFCO on 30 November 2000. Two months before that, IFFCO-Tokio had started operations. At his farewell party, Awasthi announced that he would be the financial advisor to IFFCO-Tokio from the following day.

'I had no idea. I do not know if it was his faith in me, but I did not sit idle even for twenty-four hours. It was a major event in my life. I worked for another fifteen years. I have no words to describe my regard for him,' said Tandon.

It was the practice at IFFCO to give retired personnel an annual health support of ₹5,000. When this came to Awasthi's attention, he decided to do away with this cash grant; instead, he used this sum to create a group insurance scheme for all retirees and their families.

'This had a big positive impact on the morale of IFFCO employees and retirees,' said Dr I.S. Jain, Chief Medical Consultant at IFFCO.

Good relations with the government

The fertilizer industry has to operate under stringent government controls. And IFFCO was a quasi-public sector company till 2004. Therefore, maintaining good relations with the government is a key result area for any chief executive in the sector.

'Dr Awasthi has very good relations in the government,' said N.K. Kedia, chairman of ITIS.

Awasthi had begun cultivating his connections with every level of the government from the time he had been the de facto executive assistant to Paul Pothen. He has nurtured and built those links over the years.

H.S. Bawa adds, 'He has developed very good rapport with bureaucrats, with the ministry and other concerned government officials. So, he has always been able to take care of IFFCO's interests in particular and the industry's interests in general.'

Project cleared in five minutes

The Aonla expansion was still under way when Awasthi told D.K. Bhatt, the newly appointed plant head at Phulpur, to prepare a detailed project report and submit it to the government. There were three layers of approval those days—pre-Public Investment Board (PIB), PIB and Cabinet Committee on Economic Affairs. Then, the Ministry of Environment (now the Ministry of Environment, Forest and Climate Change) gave the clearance for the project to start.

Awasthi told Bhatt in January 1995, 'There will be no pre-PIB this time. Your PIB will take place on 29 January. You have to come for the presentation.'

On the day of the PIB meeting, they first went to meet the Fertilizer Secretary who did not show much interest in the project. The Department of Expenditure and the Planning Commission were also not very keen on the project. They thought it was a loss-making proposal.

Awasthi was very upset. He said, 'We will not go for PIB approval. They are creating unnecessary obstacles. We will set up the plant without their approval.'

'No, no. That will be inappropriate,' Tandon protested.

The PIB meeting was scheduled for later that day. When the IFFCO team reached the site, they found Coal India officers being grilled over a ₹190 crore project. After an hour, the proposal was rejected, and Coal India was asked to come back six months later with a revised plan.

It was then IFFCO's turn to make its presentation. Awasthi said, 'We have already started expansion of our Aonla plant. Phulpur will be our second expansion. The project has very good profitability. We have a very good team. The plant head of Phulpur is here with us. We have always completed our projects within time and cost. We will also do this project in record time.'

To Bhatt's utter disbelief, PIB, comprising joint secretaries from five or six departments, cleared the project in five minutes flat. 'They did not raise any objection. I was stunned. It was unbelievable,' he said.

It was a testament to the esteem Awasthi commanded in official circles even in his early days as IFFCO chief executive, as well as a testament to the strength of his relationships within the government.

Spoke fearlessly to secretaries

Despite his good relations with bureaucrats across the board, or maybe because of it, he spoke truth to power.

Gahlaut calls Awasthi a very courageous man because not many people have the guts to go and tell a secretary, 'This policy will harm the industry, so please review it.'

'But,' the IPL chief said, 'he [Awasthi] would do it very diplomatically. For example, if he had to say something unpleasant, he would first create the atmosphere by saying: "Sir, you don't even ask us for tea these days. We deserve a cup of tea at least." The ice broken, Awasthi would then broach the topic gently.'

But some people still took offence. Some secretaries still said, 'What does he think of himself?'

Of the twenty-eight-odd secretaries in the Ministry of Chemicals & Fertilizers that Awasthi has had to work with, Gahlaut can think of only three with whom Awasthi had principled differences. 'He never gave in.'

He particularly remembers an incident with a very competent Secretary who wanted to do something that would have resulted in losses for IFFCO.

Awasthi said, 'I can't let IFFCO suffer losses just to accept whatever you are saying.'

The Secretary became very angry. 'Awasthi is now persona non grata. I will not allow him to enter the department,' he screamed.

But people advised him to relent. 'Awasthi also has a point. You must listen to him. It was a principled fight. There was no other consideration,' they told him.

'They met and Awasthi succeeded not only in convincing him of his point of view but also in getting concessions from him,' said Gahlaut with a hearty laugh.

Doyen of the fertilizer industry

Awasthi was the first Asian chairman of IFA. He is considered the elder statesman of the fertilizer industry. Leading industrialists who own fertilizer companies regularly come to him for advice and guidance.

'When the sector faces a problem and there is a question of how to resolve it, they always find that interacting with him and taking his advice is something that is of great value,' informs Gahlaut.

'To outsiders, IFFCO appears to be a big fish in the corporate world, but its soul is cooperative and this is the secret of its success. It was Awasthi who laid the foundations of this success,' said Sanghani.

The IFFCO managing director has good working relationships with his peer group in the industry. There was a feeling a few years ago that IFFCO was trying to leverage its position as market leader and position itself as the big brother of the industry, but such misgivings are now a thing of the past. Other CEOs appreciate IFFCO's strength and size.

Therefore, there is both cordiality and competition among them. All of them accept Awasthi's position as the doyen of the industry.

A compassionate leader

A worker in Phulpur once misbehaved with the plant head. It was a serious offence. The report reached Awasthi, and he terminated the offender immediately and was not ready to listen to anyone asking him to review his decision. Anybody who tried to intercede on behalf of the sacked man was severely reprimanded.

'He has misbehaved with my officer. I will never forgive him,' he said adamantly.

One day, Jitendra Tiwari mustered up the courage to talk to him. 'Sir, could you please give him back his job? His whole family is in distress.'

Awasthi was livid. 'You, Mr Jitendra Tiwari! Please do not discuss this.'

'I am going. But what you're doing is inhuman,' Tiwari replied and left.

It looked like curtains for the sacked worker's career at IFFCO. Then, his wife wrote Awasthi a letter. Tiwari doesn't know if she wrote the letter on her own volition or if someone advised her to do so, but it melted Awasthi. He revoked his termination, but ordered that the worker be transferred to another unit.

Brigadier Bhanu Sud, the then Chief of Security and Administration, advised him against reinstating the offender. He said, 'This will not be appropriate. It will send a wrong message.'

'Brigadier, do you want his children to die of hunger?' Awasthi replied, brushing aside his objections.

Tiwari said he has seen him in many difficult situations, but he has never seen him compromise with his principles.

An employee was caught black marketing fertilizers. Awasthi could have forgiven him had he apologized for his mistake. Instead, the employee tried to apply pressure on Awasthi through politicians and other influential people. He even approached a central minister, who had very good relations with Awasthi, to intercede on his behalf.

Awasthi was not ready to listen to anyone and terminated his services. His mistake was not the irregularities but his attempt at using outside influence. Awasthi does not tolerate any outside interference in the internal affairs of IFFCO. That is one of the reasons for its success. He has even refused requests from higher authorities to protect IFFCO's interests.

'As the leader of the officers' association, I can say that had he not handled this pressure resolutely, there could have been many wrong appointments, wrong promotions and wrong transfers. He does not budge an inch,' said Tiwari.

But if someone from within the organization—a union leader or a delegate or an employee himself or his wife or children—approaches him for something, he is very likely to accede to the request, though he may have refused the same demand had it come from higher authorities.

'As a chief executive, I cannot take a decision that may lead to a theft in the plant. If I start trying to keep everyone happy, then it is not possible. I have not been given this position just to have good relations. I have been sent to have fair relations. I work impartially and every decision of mine is transparent,' said Awasthi, explaining his philosophy.

'It is my unalterable belief that the position of chief executive—whether of an organization, of a province, of a country or of a family—should belong to those who have the ability to drink poison like Lord Shiva. He must keep the poison in his neck so that the rest of the body remains unaffected. If you involve your personal stakes then you do not deserve to be the chief executive,' he adds.

In the mid-1990s, there were reports of rising hepatitis B cases. There was no effective treatment for this disease then. A preventive vaccine called Interferon was introduced in the market. It was, however, prohibitively expensive. Each dose cost ₹1 lakh and three doses were needed for it to operate at full efficiency.

In a meeting with Awasthi, Dr Jain suggested that IFFCO pay for all employees and their families to be vaccinated with Interferon in lieu of their Diwali bonus. Awasthi heard her out and asked her to send him a proposal. Finally, he approved the vaccination proposal—and also paid the employees their Diwali bonus.

Brajesh Kumar, president of the IFFCO Employees Union, says, 'Awasthi sir is a very compassionate man but takes care to keep his compassion in check for the greater good of the organization.'

Touching thousands of lives

There aren't many corporate leaders who are equally respected in boardrooms across India and also in the fields and villages dotting the Indian countryside.

Awasthi's ability to reach out to people in distress and make a difference to their lives is an integral part of his persona. He is revered in Sathani, his native village, where the common people refer to him as 'MD Sahab'.

A woman from Sathani said, 'What can we say about MD Sahab... He is precious like a gem. He has fulfilled all our dreams. He sent us to Rishikesh and Haridwar. We saw the two holy cities and bathed in the Ganga. Our travel, food, accommodation—everything was taken care of.'

Then, when he became the managing director of IFFCO, he facilitated the formation of a self-help group (SHG) for women. 'We have acquired many new skills. The SHG gives small loans to its needy members. He gave us pressure cookers and gas stoves. There was no hospital in this area. We had to travel long distances to reach a hospital. We requested him for a hospital in the village and he got a hospital built. We get free medicines there,' she said.

'We never thought of speaking in front of a crowd, especially before male members earlier. But now, if you put us on a stage before a mic, we can speak freely,' adds another woman.

Another woman picks up from there and said, 'No one in the history of this village has been as loving and caring as he has been. Every year, he distributes free blankets in the village. Now every family has four to five blankets. When he comes with his daughters-in-law, he distributes free sarees. Everyone is happy in the village because of him. May God grant him a healthy life of a hundred years. This is our prayer.'

An elderly man joins the group. 'No one knew this village before Awasthi. I was a school teacher here and would cycle to school every day. The road linking this village to the main road used to be a dirt track. It would turn into slush during monsoons. Coming and going to and from this village was torture. It was Awasthi who converted that dirt track into a metal road,' he said.

Ram Singh adds, 'Can you name a single managing director who goes to the villages to distribute goats? Awasthi does that—in villages across India.

His greatest gift to his native village is probably the primary health centre. Two doctors come twice a week, on Wednesdays and Saturdays. Patients, from as far away as 20 kilometres, throng this centre because the medicines are genuine and are given freely.

He has also brought solar power to the village. 'The lights on the road are powered with solar energy,' said a villager.

'He gave free goats to all the poor families. He has done everything to bring prosperity to this area. As soon as he became the managing director, he started holding eye camps. A minimum of 20,000 people in Unnao district have got their cataracts removed at camps organized by IFFCO,' he adds.

In 1995, Awasthi organized the first eye camp in Sathani. He had insisted that the operations would take place in the village itself. A room of a school was sterilized and a total of fifty operations were carried out over two days. They were all successful.

Encouraged by this, IFFCO began organizing eye camps every year and conducted thousands of operations in the villages of Unnao, Awasthi's home district. Then, this campaign was extended to every district of Uttar Pradesh. Till date, about 35,000 operations have been done and not a single one has failed.

'We had organized an eye camp near the foothills of Nepal in Lakhimpur district of Uttar Pradesh. A girl with white opaque layers in both her eyes came to the camp. She was practically blind,' said Yogendra Kumar, marketing director of IFFCO.

The doctor agreed to operate on her only if her father gave an undertaking that he would bear any risk.

The father said, 'She is already blind. I will take the risk.'

'Will you believe it? The operation was successful! When the bandage was removed and she confirmed that she could see, everyone cried,' recalls Yogendra Kumar.

Awasthi also has the ability to rise above petty family rivalries to focus on the task at hand. Vir Pratap Singh, IFFCO delegate and director of Cordet, hails from a rival political family in his village.

'But Awasthi never let that affect his relations with me. He even promoted me at the cost of his own people,' he said.

'There was an AGM three to four months after he joined as managing director. I went thinking I would not meet him. But he took me by complete surprise. He enquired about me from the state marketing manager and located me. He came from behind and put his hand on my shoulder. When I turned around, I saw him smiling at me. I bent down and touched his feet. It happened spontaneously,' said Vir Pratap Singh.

Once, a girl in D.K. Bhatt's village fell from a tree and suffered a serious injury. Her father was a poor man. She required an implant that cost ₹40,000. Bhatt asked Awasthi if he could help her. He immediately asked the IFFCO Kisan Sewa Trust to sanction the funds. The limit for such aid is only ₹25,000. Awasthi got the higher amount sanctioned through a special approval from the chairman.

'I don't think anyone asking him for something legitimate has ever returned empty-handed,' said Bhatt, who retired as marketing director of IFFCO in 2009.

Eye on costs

A fortnight after appointing him as the plant head at Phulpur, Awasthi told Bhatt to submit a report for the expansion of the plant. Bhatt made a brief report and sent it to him.

He asked, 'What will be the cost of urea?'

Bhatt had not thought about that. He had been focusing only on the equipment and the machines.

'The cost of urea will be very high. Bring it down,' he ordered.

Bhatt, who had been running machines till then, had no idea about the cost of urea. He consulted people who did know and made a revised report.

'The cost is still high. Bring it down further,' Awasthi told him.

It took four to five revisions before the IFFCO chief was satisfied with the cost of urea.

He called him, and all the officers and said, 'You must remember that running a plant and setting up a new plant are two different things. You must be travel-ready if you are going to set up a new plant. Second, you finish whatever you have to do then and there. Never delay a decision and always avoid unnecessary file work.'

It was hands-on training that Bhatt never forgot.

Women's empowerment remains a core focus area

IFFCO has made great strides towards empowering women and increasing their participation in the organization, its affiliates and its member cooperative societies. The result: women's leadership has emerged very strongly in IFFDC projects, and they have more than 43 per cent participation.

In 2019, before the formation of IFFCO's new board of directors, the by-laws were amended to reserve 5 per cent seats in the RGB and one seat on the board of directors for women. So, fifty representatives in the 1,000-member RGB are women. These fifty women representatives elect a representative from among themselves to the board of directors.

Sizes up people fast

Brigadier Surinder Kumar, Senior Executive Director (Security), had been approached by the HR department in IFFCO for the position of Chief Security Officer. He said: 'I am retiring on 31 March (2015). I can join after that.' That was the sum of his interaction with IFFCO.

As the days passed, he thought he must meet Awasthi because he found it strange that he had been selected without a formal interview. He sought an appointment and went to meet him.

Awasthi was not there when Surinder Kumar entered his chamber. He had gone to the boardroom for a meeting. He walked in five minutes later, made him feel comfortable, and asked, 'Brigadier, when can you join?'

Brigadier Kumar was taken aback. He replied, 'I am retiring on 31 March. I can join from 1 April.'

Awasthi said, 'Please join.' That was the interaction. Awasthi then went back to re-join the meeting.

As a senior military officer, the brigadier had been trained to size up people and situations and take quick decisions. He instantly recognized that Awasthi was someone who could do the same—and had the authority to take decisions once he had made up his mind.

It was Brigadier Kumar who organized Awasthi's visit to the Northeast as part of IFFCO's golden jubilee celebrations. At Nathu La Pass, the IFFCO chief wrote in the visitors' book:

> IFFCO is proud of the Indian Army. We are a farmers' organization. A majority of our brothers and sisters join the Indian Army. You defend the borders of the country, and we defend the supply lines of foodgrains.
>
> Salute to our soldiers.
>
> I, as managing director of IFFCO, wish to contribute ₹10 lakh to the Army Welfare Fund. Would be happy to know where to send.
>
> U.S. Awasthi
>
> 12 April, 2017

Once he makes up his mind, he doesn't waver

'From Nathu La they returned to Gangtok where the Farmers' Co-operators' Conference was held. Awasthi met the Additional Chief Secretary of the state and initiated discussions that resulted in the formation of Sikkim IFFCO Organics Limited. The MoU was signed, the JV company was formed, and work started soon thereafter. All this happened within one year. This speaks volumes about his vision and determination. What I perceived by watching him from close quarters is that once he makes up his mind to do something, then no matter what the circumstances, he never wavers,' said Brigadier Kumar.

His initial instincts about the man were being proved correct.

Excellent raconteur with both depth and breadth of knowledge

He took Awasthi to two parties in the northeast. In Shillong, Major General Gupta, the brigadier's course mate, was the host. It was a typical army party—drinks flowing, the army band playing, waiters attending in turbans and gloves.

'We entered the party, and I introduced him. That was all. Not even once did I have to go near him. There was a Lieutenant General, our host's boss, at the party. Awasthi spent a lot of time chatting with the two generals. They sat and dined together. His conduct was just immaculate,' remembers Brigadier Kumar.

There was a similar party in Dimapur, at the residence of Lieutenant General Anil Chauhan, who went on to become director general of military operations. He collects wooden skulls. Wherever he goes, he collects them.

The Brigadier was amazed to see Awasthi knowledgeably discussing skulls with his host. He told him many things about this art and hobby. The General had a dog. Awasthi played with him for fifteen to twenty minutes. The General's wife is a good painter. Awasthi's love for paintings is well known. 'We bought one of her paintings. Then the General presented him his book on nuclear warfare. Awasthi read the book and sent him elaborate feedback—like "On such and such page, such and such things require more clarity,"' said the Brigadier.

Some people have depth of knowledge; others have breadth of knowledge. The brigadier was very impressed to see Awasthi with both. Awasthi is a very good raconteur as well. Thus, he can make interesting conversation with almost everyone he meets.

Even as he was spreading IFFCO's wings far and wide, Awasthi never lost focus on India's farmers. He lobbied with the government for the creation of Farmers Producer Organizations (FPOs), which are farmers' collectives, owned and controlled by farmers, that work as platforms to facilitate better access to markets, inputs and government services.

In 2002, the Companies Act was amended, and a provision was inserted to promote FPOs under company law following the spirit and philosophy of cooperatives.

Said Dr Bijender Singh, Chairman, NAFED, about Awasthi: 'He is a most capable administrator. He is the best in this country. He has succeeded in every sphere, be it research or farmers' services, and this is a matter of pride for the country.'

A think tank run by experts

Awasthi had always wanted to set up a trust comprising eminent experts from various fields to function as a think tank. This trust would advise IFFCO and its top management on issues that could be taken up for farmers and cooperatives in the country. It would work in the field of policy advocacy and engage with the government and press for legislations and enactments relating to its field of operations. It would also be a vehicle for some of the philanthropic and social work that IFFCO did for the upliftment of rural people.

'I thought we were far too occupied in the management of our company to focus on these issues,' he said. 'I had been discussing the idea with the board, but it took time to materialize. Finally, we drew up a comprehensive proposal, which the board approved and the IFFCO Foundation was established in 2003.'

This foundation has blazed a trail and done pioneering work in several areas, some of which were adopted by the government as flagship programmes.

'We're happy that many of our model projects are now important programmes of the government. The Swachh Bharat Abhiyan is one such example. We took up villages for complete sanitation as a model. We created the infrastructure, demonstrated the method and brought the change,' said Awasthi.

When the government launched the programme, the IFFCO Foundation donated ₹10 crore. Then, it started a drive for soil tests, trained people and set up laboratories for the purpose. This morphed into its famous 'Save the Soil' campaign in every state of the country. Now, the government has adopted it in a big way. Similarly, under IFFCO-Tokio, the foundation started very small insurance schemes for farmers and labourers. The government also started such schemes later on a large scale.

Another major achievement of the IFFCO Foundation was the revival of Alha singing, which had become all but extinct. Alha is a form of folk music that originated in the Bundelkhand region and gained popularity across large parts of Uttar Pradesh and Madhya Pradesh.

'I remember when we were children, the whole village would throng to listen to Alha. There was a Society for Alha in our district. But we realized that Alha could not be revived only by organizing functions,' said the IFFCO managing director.

The foundation transformed the Society for Alha into an academy for imparting proper training to the artistes. 'I am very happy that a number of artistes whom we trained are actively involved in singing and are doing good work in maintaining the popularity of the art form,' he said.

IFFCO also took up the Energy Savings Project in 2003. Awasthi has always believed in conserving resources. He also believes in Mahatma Gandhi's immortal lines: 'Nature has enough resources to satisfy everyone's need, but it cannot satisfy everyone's greed.' This thinking was based on ancient Indian wisdom that the universe is one. 'To think that this is mine and that is yours is petty. The savings you make on this earth are for entire humanity,' said Awasthi. 'The government had set new norms for energy consumption in plants. The time to achieve those parameters was later relaxed but we completed it within the time period prescribed earlier,' said Awasthi.

'We keep adopting new technologies. We are not afraid of change.

Today, there is one technology, tomorrow another technology will come; we will adopt that, too. It is not important that we earn a profit from this exercise. That is immaterial. What is important is that there should be savings of resources in the country,' he said quite emphatically.

Shrilal Shukla Smriti IFFCO Sahitya Samman

Shrilal Shukla was a famous Hindi litterateur and best-selling author. His novel *Raag Darbari* is a classic on farmers and village life. 'The IFFCO board instituted the Shrilal Shukla Smriti IFFCO Sahitya Samman in his memory,' said Yogendra Kumar. It is given every year to a Hindi writer whose writings reflect the rural agricultural life of India. The awardee is presented with a memento and a cash prize of ₹11 lakh. Twelve writers have been honoured till 2022.

Awasthi remembers his father-in-law very fondly.

'Papa was a great man and a dear friend too. Our discussions used to be more on contemporary matters than on literature. He was very knowledgeable, witty and courageous,' he said.

Shrilal Shukla had joined the Uttar Pradesh Provincial Services in 1947 and was later promoted to the IAS cadre. He wrote *Raag Darbari* in 1960 and submitted it to the government for permission to publish it. The government did not give permission for eight years. In 1968, he went to the Chief Secretary and said, 'Give me permission to publish or accept my resignation.'

It was a brave and bold statement and could have backfired badly, but it worked. The government gave him the permission, and the book was published. It was an instant hit. The very next year, he was given the Sahitya Akademi Award. Later, he was awarded the Jnanpith Award and honoured with the Padma Bhushan.

'The larger objective of the Shrilal Shukla Smriti Samman is to promote quality writing on rural India, on farmers and on village life,' said Awasthi. That's the magic of Awasthi. He has this wonderful ability to create opportunities to promote a cause.

A scrupulously fair man with an eye for talent

He also has a rare ability to spot talent—and find qualities in people they themselves don't know they have.

Awasthi had gone to Phulpur in 1999 and had stayed there for two to three days. While going around the plant, he said, 'Stocks are piling up. Sales are not happening.' Bhatt, who was the plant head, had a long discussion with him on how sales could be improved.

'Shall I transfer you to marketing?' Awasthi asked. He had said this earlier on another occasion as well.

'If you think I can handle marketing, then I am ready.'

IFFCO was under the government's control then; so, Bhatt needed to go through an interview board. Awasthi prepared him for the interview. He selected his suit, decided the colour of the tie and coached him on now to answer the questions. When Bhatt went to meet him before the interview, he embraced him and said, 'Go; you will be selected.'

That's how Bhatt, a mechanical engineer who had spent all his life in plant maintenance, became the marketing director of IFFCO. 'That is the talent of Awasthi. He can turn someone into something else and get things done by him,' said a grateful Bhatt, who retired in 2009.

Awasthi has also earned a formidable reputation for being scrupulously fair in all his dealings.

During his stint as acting CMD of RCF, PDIL, a public sector company, had mistakenly quoted ₹8 lakh for a contract worth ₹15 lakh. S.P. Sharma, the CMD of PDIL, met Awasthi and explained the situation to him.

Awasthi said, 'No problem, I will give you ₹15 lakh.'

The accounts and purchase departments raised a hue and cry over this. They said it was against procedure and precedent. Awasthi told them,

'It's all right. It's a government company. They have mistakenly quoted a wrong amount. Why should we cause them a loss?'

Awasthi does all his business with the highest ethical standards. In the fertilizer market, there is a system of giving off-season rebates for down payments. Usually, thirty days' credit is given, but if someone makes a down payment, he/she is given a discount. This facility is withdrawn when the peak season arrives.

But IFFCO gives this discount even in the peak season. 'We all argued that there is no need to give discounts in the peak season. The demand is so high that people sell fertilizers in the black market,' said Kamal Verma.

But Awasthi was firm. 'No, this is our system, and we will not change it.'

'This has created trust in IFFCO. Farmers and dealers alike wait for IFFCO fertilizers to arrive,' said Verma, with the benefit of hindsight.

It isn't just cooperatives and farmers that Awasthi stands by. According to H.S. Bawa, with whom he has worked very closely for decades, 'He is a very good friend to have.'

He further adds, 'If he is your friend, then he is your friend forever. He will always stand by you. That's a big trait because if you can trust each other then there can be nothing better than that. And in his own way, he is quite modest. He tried to show at times that he is a big boss, but he is generally very modest.'

Foreign exchange losses

Kamal Verma came back from his posting in Oman in 2009. IFFCO had suffered heavy losses in foreign exchange in the initial months of the year. Verma was new to the foreign exchange market and had no idea about how the dollar would move. IFFCO had very high foreign exchange exposure because its Paradeep and Kandla plants are dependent on imported raw materials.

Awasthi was very anxious about the losses. He was bargaining very hard on the prices of IFFCO's imports, but the fluctuations in foreign exchange were nullifying all his hard work.

One day, he called Verma and said angrily, 'Will you drown IFFCO?'

Verma could not sleep that night. It was a difficult and tricky situation for him—a misjudgement of even one paisa could lead to a loss of ₹10,000 on a ₹10 lakh transaction. 'Imagine the consequences if you misjudge the movement, even by a rupee. Our daily payments were in the range of ₹4 crore to ₹5 crore. So, the losses could be very high [...] But if your judgement was right, you could also earn as much,' he said.

IFFCO had run up losses of ₹60 crore to ₹70 crore because of foreign exchange fluctuations. The dollar had been steady at around ₹48 those days. There were days when the rupee actually appreciated against the US currency.

'I was new to the foreign exchange market and used to take forward cover to save ourselves from the fluctuations. A consultant we had engaged with told the Joint MD that taking forward cover when the rupee was stable was losing us money,' said Verma.

The joint managing director asked Verma and informed Awasthi about this.

A day after excoriating him, Awasthi called him and said, 'Whenever you have any doubts, come to me directly. We will discuss together and make a strategy.'

Verma proudly said, 'It has been nine years since that day, and we have earned profits on our foreign exchange transactions every year after that.'

Fight with a foreign consultant

Haldor Topsoe of Denmark was the technology supplier of the ammonia plant at Phulpur. When it was being expanded, they had sent an engineer to oversee the process. He was not comfortable with Bhatt and would always object to whatever he decided.

Since Bhatt was the plant head, everyone followed his instructions.

The foreign engineer told Awasthi that Bhatt was working with complete disregard for norms and procedures. 'There could be an accident at the plant,' he complained.

A livid Awasthi summoned Bhatt and sought an explanation. The engineer had also come to the head office that day. He was sitting in the visitors' chamber.

Awasthi said, 'There is lack of coordination between the contractor and IFFCO personnel. This can impede the smooth functioning of the project and later, the plants, so please learn to cooperate.' He was visibly angry.

'Who will you catch if anything goes wrong?' Bhatt replied.

This forthright and honest answer changed Awasthi's manner completely. He instantly became normal.

'All right, you go and meet the Director, Technical,' he said.

Bhatt went to the visitors' chamber and confronted the foreign engineer. He told him that carrying tales would not work if he expected cooperation from him.

The engineer fell in line after that.

Love for IFFCO over all else

Awasthi completed twenty-five years as managing director of IFFCO on 1 February 2018. The union leaders had wanted to organize a grand function to celebrate the occasion. They had also moved this proposal at a board meeting.

But Awasthi shot down the suggestion. 'The institution is bigger than the person,' he said.

Finally, a small function was organized at the head office where the leaders poured their hearts out in praise of Awasthi. Everyone had something special to say about him.

'His love for IFFCO is unparalleled,' said Balwant Singh, General Secretary of the IFFCO Officers' Association in Delhi, and recounts an incident from long ago—1992, when IFFCO had turned twenty-five. The IFFCO management had not shown any interest in celebrating the silver jubilee.

M.K. Bhardwaj was the leader of the union in which Balwant Singh was involved. 'We decided to organize a cultural night to celebrate the occasion,' he said.

Awasthi was then the CMD of PPCL. Its corporate office was a short walking distance from IFFCO House in Nehru Place. Balwant Singh had accompanied Bhardwaj for a meeting with Awasthi. 'He gave ₹5,000 from his pocket and booked the auditorium in the SCOPE building for the function,' he said.

'He may be X's friend; or he may be Y's friend; and Z may claim he is very close to him. He [Awasthi] will meet everyone; he will be nice to everyone. But if anyone suggests something that is even remotely, obliquely detrimental to IFFCO, he will reject it, even if that suggestion, request or pressure comes from the highest quarters,' said P.S. Gahlaut.

He adds that Awasthi is by nature a very considerate man. But he can be ruthless and nasty with people who, attracted by his position and his ability to do things, try to be too clever by half.

And like very successful people, he has friends and detractors in equal measure. Gahlaut, who has seen both the positive and the negative sides of Awasthi, adds that he can sometimes come across as a bundle of contradictions.

'If someone tells you that he has not seen anyone better than Awasthi, that he goes out of his way to help people, that he takes care of even those lower down in the hierarchy, he is 100 per cent correct. But you will also meet people who will say Awasthi is an egoist, he behaves as if he is the greatest man on earth, he is not ready to listen to anybody—and those people will also be correct,' said the managing director of IPL.

Kamal Verma, who has worked with Awasthi for almost three decades, said his boss is like a coconut—tough outside, but extremely soft inside, full of compassion.

TEN

A LIFETIME, A COOPERATIVE

Awasthi maintained a furious pace, visiting as many as 125 locations, over one year during 2016–2017 as part of IFFCO's golden jubilee celebrations. With some variations because of local factors, the theme of his speeches was similar everywhere. He very succinctly recapitulated IFFCO's journey over the past fifty years, elucidated his vision for its future and advised the gathered farmers on how to improve their lives and livelihoods.

Addressing the Annual Co-operators' Conference (2017) in Shri Krishna Memorial Hall, near the famous Gandhi Maidan in Patna, he said: 'Our beginning was very small. No one believed that something good and worthwhile can happen in the cooperative sector. I remember when I offered suggestions people used to say, "*Arey, aap log to sahkarita wale hain, kha peekar chale jayenge* [People who run cooperatives…you will make money and disappear]." We have proved them wrong. Today, IFFCO has assets worth ₹50,000 crore. It is your ₹425 crore which has grown to ₹50,000 crore today. [This value has grown further since then; as of 31 March 2022, it was ₹1.06 lakh crore on an equity base of ₹634 crore.] This is your money. We are the custodians…'

'The twenty-first century is characterized by speed. It is the age of fast communication. But our cooperative societies are still carrying loads of files and moving at a snail's pace. You will not survive if you do not adopt technology. Therefore, in this fiftieth year, IFFCO has taken up the task of connecting all our member societies and their members with the ICDP. If you give your mobile number and your Aadhaar number, you can get connected to the platform. We have 36,000 member societies; very soon, this number will rise to 50,000. That means we will have five crore people connected to the platform. You can sell your produce to customers in any part of the country at the price you want…

'You do not get competitive prices for your produce because the middleman takes most of the profit. This digital platform enables you to completely bypass the middlemen. That's why we have undertaken this huge endeavour with the belief that we will have your cooperation and support, and we will be successful…

'We manufacture chemical fertilizers, but we are against their rampant application. Excessive use of urea is spoiling your soil. Today, you make a vow that you will use 25 per cent less urea. If you apply four bags of urea, then I recommend you use one bag less, and in its place, use compost and green manure. You will save money. Your crop will have less pests. The soil will also require less water…

'Global warming is a real thing. We have unseasonal rains. We have very high temperatures at the time of sowing. When rains are needed, there are no showers. So, its effect is very severe, especially on farmers. But we have a solution. We have a tree in our country, the neem tree. It has exceptional powers…

'Last year [2015–2016], we planted 13 lakh neem trees. We are always ready to buy nimauli at ₹15 per kg. You bring it to the nearest IFFCO office. They will pay you immediately. This year, we will plant 26 lakh neem trees. We will give you saplings free of cost. But you will have to care for them like your children. They will then grow and give you clean air. They will also become your source of income. The warming atmosphere will cool. We will have better weather, more rains, better crops, and better life…'

Awasthi counselled like a mentor, admonished like a guardian and regaled like a friend. When he finished, he was given a standing ovation.

These speeches, in many ways, encapsulated Awasthi's relationship with India's farmers and the close connection he shares with them. His concern for their well-being is genuine, his outreach to them is pragmatic and his vision for their future is attainable and sustainable. There is also a very visible strain of paternalistic altruism characterizing Awasthi's connection with India's farmers.

The three deaths that disturbed him

The year 2011 was a difficult one for both IFFCO and Awasthi. There were three deaths, one after the other. First, IFFCO's Chairman Surinder Jakhar died in a freak accident. He was cleaning his pistol when it went off, leaving him dead on the spot. Then in April, N.K Bhardwaj, president of the IFFCO Employees' Union, died of cardiac arrest while holding a meeting in the head office. The third tragedy occurred in October when Shrilal Shukla, noted litterateur and Awasthi's father-in-law, passed away.

'I am on that plane where any sorrow is momentary. I never look back in life. I always look forward. I am an optimist. I had wonderful relations with all three. I still remember them. When I remember them, I have a feeling of hollowness, but that is all. It does not affect me,' he said with a phlegmatic sigh.

Awasthi had excellent relations with everyone, but Jakhar's death was like the loss of a family member. His thinking matched with that of Awasthi's—he was a great agriculturist and his heart always beat for farmers. They did several projects together. The tragedy was a great loss to the organization, and India lost a great agriculturist and a cooperative leader. In his memory, IFFCO has named its Paradeep unit's township as Surinder Jakhar Nagar. There is one Surinder Jakhar Complex at Gurgaon as well.

'The void he has left is exceedingly difficult to fill. It was made worse by a very speculative story in a magazine that alleged his death was a murder and not an accident. It was a baseless story, which nobody believed. It came and disappeared. I don't know why it was written,' said Awasthi, his disgust showing even after a decade.

'Mr Bhardwaj was a much-loved employee of IFFCO. He was the president of the union at our head office, and the chief coordinator of all the unions in IFFCO. Every employee in IFFCO looked up to him and respected him,' said Awasthi. In keeping with IFFCO's tradition, the company has named a garden in Phulpur after him.

Regarding his father-in-law, he said he was not really an admirer of his works and read his books only because his mother and sister had written to him about them. 'So, I thought I must read the book before he comes,' said Awasthi with a sheepish smile.

Awasthi was only two or three years old when his father passed away. His elder brother, Dr Devi Shanker Awasthi, took the place of his father. 'After his death, I felt very lonely. Shrilal Shukla filled this void with his affection and love. I sometimes feel very fortunate for having had a forty-year-long association with him. I had developed a memorable bond with Papa, who influenced me in many ways with his thoughts,' he said.

In 1983, Awasthi was offered a job as general manager at a methanol plant in Malaysia. The salary was tempting—$10,000 per month. His mother, who was living with him at that time, and his wife, were not in favour of him taking up the job.

'Papa-Mummy also came to our place then and, in a conversation, Papa read a Sanskrit shloka, which means, "What is the use of that property that relatives and friends cannot use and seeing which enemies do not get jealous?" I decided then and there that I would not take up this job. I never thought about it again,' he said. Today, he understands that his decision, based on Shrilal Shukla's opinion, was good for himself, his society, the farming community and his country.

Once, his father-in-law questioned, somewhat philosophically, the way the law of the land is administered when the accused standing in court does not understand a single word of what is said—either against him or in his defence. At the conclusion of the hearing, the judgement, too, is then pronounced in a language of which he is completely ignorant.

This set Awasthi thinking.

'Perhaps this is the biggest drawback in our beloved country. This is what was in my mind while preparing the Agriculture Portal in IFFCO. This is why we make information available to the farmer in his own language,' he explains.

On another occasion, Shrilal Shukla asked: 'What does democracy mean to the poor? What is *his* advantage in a democracy?'

Awasthi kept thinking about this for several days—about how to benefit the common man, the farmer of the country. After much deliberation, he decided that IFFCO should form a general insurance company and try to connect poor farmers with the organization.

'That was what led to the birth of IFFCO-Tokio General Insurance Company. We launched the Sankat Haran Insurance Scheme, which gives the farmer the benefit of personal accident insurance on buying fertilizers. With this scheme, crores of farmers are getting the benefit of free insurance,' said Awasthi. With the death of his father-in-law, Awasthi lost a wise sounding board. Many of the above issues have been exclusively tackled by our government, led by Prime Minister Modi.

These three deaths, coming close on the heels of each other, drove home for Awasthi the fact that all humans are mortals.

Embracing the new anew

January 1st is a special day in IFFCO. That day, anyone can meet Awasthi without an appointment. One can simply walk into his chamber and discuss whatever they want with him.

It is a tradition at IFFCO for Awasthi to address the New Year's Day function. The function on 1 January 2018 was special as he would be attending a function after a gap of three to four years. Addressing the gathering of union leaders and IFFCO employees, he said: 'A year ends and a new year begins. There is always a link between what is ending and what is beginning. That link is our resolve and our endeavours, inspired by our strong willpower. It is the willpower of its people that takes a society to glorious heights. If we look at the history of mankind, we find that behind our evolution as human beings or as countries, there is always a connecting link. Everyone wants his child to be better than him. Everybody makes sacrifices in the present for a better future.

'We completed fifty years in 2017. We are now on the threshold of a new beginning. We must figure out how we can contribute to the growth of our country through the growth of IFFCO. Fifty-one years ago, when we started out on our professional journey, things were quite different from what they are today. Whether it was setting up the plants or running them or how we did the marketing—everything has been changing continuously. But history repeats itself, and the same things come back to us again, albeit in different forms.

'The twenty-first century is a digital century. In this century, humans will have to compete with machines powered by artificial intelligence. A massive challenge is around the corner for large organizations and for countries with large populations. There is a region in Saudi Arabia, called Aqaba. Its location is very strategic. It borders Israel, Egypt, Jordan and Syria. They are developing a 26,000 square kilometres business hub there called "Neome," where everything will be managed by robots and artificial intelligence. There will be no fossil fuel. All the required energy will be generated from unconventional sources. This is an experiment that will be successful. The project's cost is $500 billion.'

'The idea of developing human capital has taken a back seat there because they have a small population who live in a relatively large area. They do not want expatriates to go and work there. Every country is trying to secure itself, whether it is America or China or Saudi Arabia or Iran or India. When we talk about "Make in India," America talks about "Make in America."'

'I met more than two lakh farmers during the golden jubilee campaign across the country. Everyone had the same complaint, that, while we can produce anything, where can we sell them? After so many years, we have not been able to create a market that gives farmers' adequate income. This is an incomprehensible malady. Our farmers are better than the farmers of many other countries. We have not been able to change our system according to changes in the circumstances. We created government *mandis* with the goal that the government will buy the agricultural produce from farmers. We appointed agents in the *mandis* to purchase the produce. These agents soon started exploiting farmers in a new form. We started giving subsidies, but could not develop a system where the subsidies could go to the targeted beneficiaries. They mostly go to those who do not need them. So, a distortion has crept into the system.

'In IFFCO, we have continuously tried to be in step with changing times and technologies. I do not know how many of you were there when I joined IFFCO as managing director in 1993. I was not here from 1986 to 1993. The Government of India had appointed me the chairman of PPCL. When I came back in 1993, I saw the same old technology was still being used—the same telex, the same items, the same old-fashioned typewriters. There had been no change in the system. Imagine where we would have been had we kept following those same systems? We adopted modern technology and kept changing it as the technology changed. The same set of people created new systems.

'Recently, I had an interaction with colleagues from IFFCO-Tokio. About 5,000 people are working there. I told them that digital marketing is now the new idea, so you should do it. In the last three months, the digital group has sold policies worth ₹80 crore. Their cost of marketing is 4 per cent. Traditional marketing incurs a cost of 20 per cent. This difference, of 16 per cent, will have an enormous impact on the prices of policies. The consumer will go to those who sell their policies at a cheaper rate. Now, Amazon is thinking of entering the insurance business. Obviously, its policies will have lower premiums. You will ask: how will it provide services? The answer is: it will outsource services.

'So, we will have to be agile. We will have to be at our best always. Our plants are efficient. We must make our marketing more efficient. We must spruce up our delivery system. We must adopt digital marketing in a big way, and consolidate IFFCO eBazar. The market for seeds has enormous potential. IFFDC is doing excellent work there. We have been able to check the sale of fake agrochemicals in the market. Now, we must consolidate our position in the market.

'There are many challenges and there are tremendous opportunities. Together we will face the challenges and together we will grab the opportunities. I, once again, express my best wishes to you and your family members for a wonderful new year. Be healthy, be happy and have a blissful life. Thank you very much.'

The speech lasted about twenty minutes and was again a mix of sound management lessons, paternalistic advice and a peep into the future. Awasthi was clearly laying out the roadmap for the future. Those who can keep pace with his vision are welcome; those who cannot, will need to be helped. That was the message he was giving his stakeholders.

Even the most dynamic and successful people have to face their own share of adversities and challenges.

From July 2019 to May 2021, Awasthi had his home and office raided by different investigative agencies. However, it has not deterred him from his commitment to farmers, cooperatives and the country. He launched new-generation fertilizers like nano-urea (liquid) and nano-DAP (liquid). Under his guidance and supervision, IFFCO developed six high-yield varieties of neem plants (FRI-IFFCO 1-6). He established the Nano Bio Research Centre at Kalol, Gujrat. IFFCO had acquired a scientific company in the South for research and innovation. Under his leadership, IFFCO has broken all its previous records by touching the pre-tax profit figure at ₹4000 crore during FY 2022–2023.

When asked how he can keep his balance amidst all these odds, Awasthi says with a smile, 'I have no ill will towards anyone, these are all professional hazards.'

India still dependent on foreign technology

India is the second-largest consumer of fertilizers in the world, but the Indian fertilizer industry is still dependent on imported technology. This is an anomaly that bothers Awasthi, and he has a somewhat simplistic explanation for this. 'The desire to travel abroad is so high in our country that people do not want our own technology to develop. We pay many times more to foreign professionals than to our own people just because in this system there are opportunities to travel abroad,' he said, oblivious to the fact that most Indian companies do not invest at all in R&D and are happy with whatever technology they can buy abroad.

But Awasthi passionately believes that but for the temptation to go abroad, India would have developed indigenous technology long ago. 'In the fertilizer industry, PDIL was the right choice for technology transfer, but PDIL got involved in catalyst manufacturing and many other things,' he said.

Awasthi feels that PDIL should have been made a strong technology group, and its employees should have been paid good salaries. He had suggested to the authorities that instead of government control over technology companies like PDIL, fertilizer companies should be allowed to buy PDIL. Then, PDIL could acquire all the technologies and work closely with the industry. This would have been the best and most effective method for technology to be transferred. But the government did not like this idea.

Luc Maene, the long-serving former director general of IFA, however, lauds the Indian fertilizer industry for its efficiency and safety record. 'In terms of safety, security, efficiency and output, it is among the best in the world. You look at the plant in Kalol. This plant is forty years old. It's spick and span. It's like a new plant. It's extremely well maintained. It has very good technical people,' he said. He adds that there is nothing wrong with Indian engineers, there is nothing wrong with the way plants are being run, but India still imports massive amounts of fertilizers.

This, he feels, is not sustainable.

Government is just a system; it depends on its people

The IFFCO managing director has strong opinions on the government and how it works. Having spent a lifetime working closely with the government, he has often had a ringside seat when important, era-defining decisions were being taken. This has given him insights that many others do not have.

'The government is just a system,' he said. 'Government officials and employees bring it alive. So, support, opposition, or indifference depends on the people working there. I have met people from whom I have got extraordinary support. I've also met people who were not supportive, as well as those who were indifferent. There were also people who opposed my initiatives and created obstacles. I have met *all* kinds of people. Just as you meet all kinds of people in life, in the same way, you meet diverse types of people in every phase of your business,' he adds, his wisdom backed by more than five decades of experience.

Awasthi has had the opportunity to observe several politicians across India from very close quarters. 'They are the same everywhere,' he said. 'They are all very smart people, many times more intelligent and smarter than us.'

According to Awasthi, it took a lot of time for people to understand economic reforms. 'In a democracy, it's not like you push the button and the light comes on. It takes time to restructure the way the government works. But the reforms process has sped up decision-making in the government,' he said.

All in a day's work

Like many successful people, Awasthi too has had to face his share of adversities and challenges. Between July 2019 and May 2021, Awasthi had his home and office raided by different investigating agencies. However, these raids could not deter him from his commitment to India's farmers, her cooperatives and the country. He launched new-generation fertilizers like nano-urea (liquid) and nano-DAP (liquid). Under his guidance and supervision, IFFCO developed six high-yield varieties of neem plants (FRI-IFFCO1-6). He established the Nano Bio Research Centre at Kalol, Gujarat. IFFCO also acquired a scientific company in South India to help it with research and innovation. Under his leadership, IFFCO has broken all its previous profit records by touching a pre-tax profit figure of ₹4106 crore during 2022–2023.

When asked how he keeps his balance amidst all these odds, Awasthi says with a smile: 'I have no ill will towards anyone. These are all professional hazards.'

Elder statesman of a global industry

The little village boy who would take the attendance of workers who were double his size and several times his age, has transformed into the elder statesman of the global fertilizer industry and has emerged as an internationally renowned figure.

Charlotte Habebrand, the director general of IFA, said there are very few larger-than-life figures in the world of fertilizers, and Awasthi is definitely one of them.

'IFA annual meetings are attended by about 1,400 persons from across the globe. I would say every single one of them would know the name of Mr Awasthi. No matter what their rank, no matter what their position in their company. I don't know if that's the case with many other individuals in the fertilizer industry. Everybody knows his name,' she said. Also, no other fertilizer company in the world enjoys the same level of recognition. 'If you ask somebody in Canada or the US about Agriem, or Mosaic, people may not know. But here in India, everybody knows IFFCO. This is tremendous, more so because it's a cooperative,' said Habebrand.

That could be Awasthi's greatest achievement that he has transformed IFFCO—which is a cooperative, a body not listed on the stock exchanges and not part of any glamorous industry—into a household name in India.

EPILOGUE

Awasthi has now led IFFCO for almost three decades. During this time, he has transformed a cooperative fertilizer company into the world's largest conglomerate, spanning twenty-one companies. He has trained, mentored and nurtured a talented pool of senior managers who could take over from him when he decides to hang up his boots, but Awasthi is not yet thinking of walking into the sunset.

The boy from a nondescript village in Uttar Pradesh is now a respected international figure in the fertilizer industry. Like many successful professionals, he has a larger-than-life personality. But behind the successful professional, what is Awasthi like as a person?

In his own words: 'I was born in a village. My father died when I was still a little boy; so, I grew up with very little parental support. As a result, I always felt I was living on someone else's kindness. 'At the same time, we had the fortune of being quietly and intelligently guided by a woman of great foresight—my mother, Durgavati Awasthi. She made us what we are today. She allowed us to grow organically. My mother realized that I harboured a deep sense of sorrow—of having to live without the protection of a father in what was still a man's world.

'It was the deep sense of resentment that made me take command of whatever situation I found myself in, and to give directions to others, regardless of their age or stature. I always felt I was born to lead, and I must lead from the front. As I grew older, I started refining and harnessing my capabilities. But it was when I joined BHU that I realized the importance of my country and its farmers. I had found the two causes that would remain my lifelong passions. I also realized, within a few years of starting my professional life, that I could achieve my dreams only on the platform of cooperatives.'

An inspirational leader, Awasthi was chosen to be the CMD of PPCL in 1986. There is no looking back since then. He charted his own path and overcame several managerial, economic and technological limitations with innovations that made for out-of-the-box solutions. Throughout his professional life, he neither has had any ill will for nor blindly followed anyone.

He has worked under the regimes of nine prime ministers, from Rajiv Gandhi to Narendra Modi. During this period, he faced good, indifferent as well as bad times, but eventually, he garnered the support of every government because, regardless of their attitude, he worked tirelessly for the best of his country, farmers and cooperatives.

Awasthi's professional journey started in 1967 with the creation of chemical fertilizers. But, in 2010, he realized that these were damaging the soil. Hence, he started looking at alternatives. He is credited with launching the 'Save the Soil' campaign in which he and his colleagues promoted the use of a combination of organic and chemical fertilizers. Initially, it did not get much response. Then, he started thinking about using nano-technology in agriculture.

With that basic idea in mind, he initiated research and mentored scientists that enabled IFFCO to launch nano-urea (liquid) on 1 August 2021. Then, on 20 October 2022, his team also produced nano-DAP on a commercial scale. These are revolutionary products, not only in the Indian context but also on a global scale. They are environmentally friendly—they do not have any negative impact on air and water. Their use will help improve the quality of the soil.

Awasthi has been blessed with colleagues who admire him and his vision of creating a better world for his country. He is particularly thankful for the contributions of R.P. Singh and Yogendra Kumar and to his long-serving secretary, R.K. Chawla, and Raj Kumar, who looked after his house. He is also grateful to Dr Indu Jain, whose guidance has helped him maintain good health.

Awasthi is a 'People's CEO' who firmly believes in taking everyone along, especially by empowering farmers who, in turn, will result in a prosperous India.

He adds: 'I express my gratitude to my bhabhi Kamlesh Awasthi for her blessings since childhood. I would also like to thank my younger sister, Dr Rekha Awasthi, who always stood by me in any situation. I also thank my family members who always tolerated me despite my lack of time, but they all know how much I love them. I also thank my wife, Rekha Awasthi; her cool and composed behaviour has helped me retain my sanity during difficult times. Lastly, I thank all my friends who have been there for me.' This book is an attempt to encapsulate his life, personal and professional, as he continues to serve as the MD and CEO at IFFCO. In his own words, 'I have no regrets in life, and if given a chance, I would like to be born again in this beautiful country and would like to serve Bharat Mata forever.'

A LIFE EXTRAORDINAIRE

1986 Joined Pyrites Phosphates & Chemicals Limited (PPCL), a Government of India undertaking, as the Managing Director.

1987 Cleared the long-pending ropeway project for PPCL's rock phosphate mines near Mussoorie immediately after joining.

Acquired additional 40 acres of land and commenced construction of sulphuric acid and pyrite-based single super phosphate (SSP) project in record time.

Persuaded the Government of India to reverse its decision to retrench 1,200 employees of PPCL.

1988 Launched the SoneGanga brand and commenced the seedling programme.

1989 Commissioned the phosphoric acid and SSP plant on schedule.

1990 Introduced trading of imported fertilizers as a part of a competitive business strategy.

1991 Appointed chairman-cum-managing director (CMD) of Rashtriya Chemicals and Fertilizers Limited (RCF) in addition to his assignment as CMD, PPCL.

1992 Empowered the officers of RCF by publishing the Powers of Officers, which helped in the decentralization of power, thereby leading to speedy decision-making.

1993 Joined as Managing Director of Indian Farmers Fertiliser Cooperative Limited (IFFCO) on February 1. Established the Indian Farm Forestry Development Cooperative Limited (IFFDC) with the objective of implementing afforestation projects, undertaking projects in farm forestry, and wasteland development at the village level and improving the socio-economic status of the rural poor, tribal communities and women in particular.

1994 Streamlined existing systems and procedures, made them transparent and empowered officers to raise the morale of the workforce.

1995 Envisioned and conceived Vision 2000 for IFFCO and began implementing it to get the cooperative ready for the new millennium.

Helmed the expansion projects at Aonla and Phulpur units and a revamp project at the Kalol unit during 1993–1997, resulting in a doubling of the total installed capacity of urea from 4,900 metric tons per day (MTPD) to 9,750 MTPD.

1996 Successfully commissioned the Aonla Expansion Project, thereby doubling the urea production capacity of the plant from 7,26,000 metric tons per annum (MTPA) to 14,52,000 MTPA.

Established IFFCO's first biofertilizer plant at Phulpur, Uttar Pradesh.

1997 First Asian to be elected as President of the International Fertilizer Association (IFA).

Successfully commissioned the Phulpur Expansion Project, thereby increasing the urea production capacity of the unit from 4,95,000 MTPA to 12,21,000 MTPA.

Successfully completed the Kalol Revamp Project, thereby increasing the plant's urea production capacity from 3,96,000 MTPA to 5,44,500 MTPA.

1998 Addressed the delegates at United Nations (UN) Headquarters, New York, on 29 April 1998. A collection of patriotic poems and songs 'Azadi ki Agnishikaen' was published.

1999 Successfully commissioned the Kandla Expansion Project, increasing the plant's complex fertilizer production capacity from 13,06,000 MTPA to 16,00,000 MTPA.

2000 Decided to diversify into the general insurance sector. Entered into a joint venture agreement with Tokio Marine and Fire Insurance Company, Japan; IFFCO-Tokio General Insurance Company Limited set up.

Entered into a joint venture agreement for Oman India Fertilizer Company (OMIFCO) in Oman.

2001 Set up Kisan Sewa Trust in the wake of the Gujarat earthquake. The trust provides relief and rehabilitation to the victims of natural calamities and provides medical aid to the rural poor.

2002 IFFCO by-laws amended following the enactment of the Multi State Cooperative Societies Act 2002 to enable repatriation of Government of India equity.

Took initiative to double the production capacity of Industries Chimiques Du Senegal, Senegal, from 3,30,000 tonne P2Os to 6,60,000 tonne P2Os per annum.

2003 Commenced repatriation of Government of India (GoI) equity in IFFCO.

IFFCO Foundation established as a trust with the objective of promoting cooperative development, enhancing capacities and capabilities of human resources and the technical and business competence of cooperatives, etc.

2004 Completed repatriation of entire GoI equity, making IFFCO a cooperative wholly owned by cooperative societies in July 2004.

Set up IFFCO Kisan Logistics Ltd. as a wholly owned subsidiary of IFFCO for diversifying into logistics.

Invested in the equity of National Commodity and Derivative Exchange Ltd.

2005 Set up Kisan International Trading FZE, Dubai (KIT), a wholly owned subsidiary of IFFCO in Dubai, for international trading and investment.

Acquired the sick Phosphoric Fertiliser Complex at Paradeep, Odisha, from Oswal Chemicals & Fertilizers Limited, and turned it around. With this acquisition, IFFCO increased its all-India complex fertilizer production capacity from 24,15,000 MTPA to 43,35,000 MTPA in 2005–2006.

Launched a massive energy-saving project at ammonia and urea plants in Kalol, Phulpur and Aonla in two phases to upgrade the existing plant technology, bring down the energy consumption levels and make its plants more energy efficient to reduce the subsidy outgo of GoI.

2006 Carbon dioxide recovery (CDR) projects were implemented at Aonla and Phulpur units to reduce carbon footprint and meet the CO_2 deficit created by feed/fuel changeover from naphtha to gas at the Phulpur unit and additional demand of CO_2 for additional urea production at the Aonla unit. IFFCO was the first in the country to adopt this technology within the urea industry.

2007 Diversified into rural telephony and established a joint venture company called IFFCO Kisan Sanchar Limited, in collaboration with Star Global and Airtel.

2008 Established a joint venture company in Jordan in collaboration with Jordan Phosphate Mines Company for setting up a phosphoric acid plant called Jordan India Fertiliser Company.

Set up a special economic zone in Nellore by incorporating a wholly-owned subsidiary called IFFCO Kisan SEZ Ltd.

2009 Initiated the Soil Rejuvenation Programme through the 'Save the Soil Campaign'.

2010 Acquired equity stake in Growmax Resources Corporation, Canada, and its subsidiary Growmax Agri Corp., Canada, which is involved in the exploration of near-surface phosphates, potash brine and other minerals, and potential development of fertilizer projects in the Bayovar region of Peru.

2011 Diversified into e-commerce and supply chain by setting up a wholly owned subsidiary called IFFCO eBazar Ltd.

Set up the country's first water-soluble fertilizer plant at Kandla with a capacity of 15,000 MTPA of urea phosphate.

2012 Set up a zinc sulphate monohydrate plant at Kandla with an installed capacity of 30,000 MTPA.

2013 Commissioned the captive barge jetty at Kandla for handling raw materials.

2015 Diversified into agrochemicals by setting up a joint venture called IFFCO-MC Crop Science Pvt. Ltd., in collaboration with Mitsubishi Corporation Ltd., Japan.

Initiated R&D activities with Forest Research Institute, Dehradun, for the production of good quality neem to improve the quality and availability of neem oil. 'Neem Plantation Campaign' was undertaken across all states in India.

2016 Set up IFFCO Global Enterprises Limited.

2017 Diversified into rural financing by setting up a joint venture called IFFCO Kisan Finance Limited.

2018 Set up Sikkim IFFCO Organics Ltd. in partnership with the Government of Sikkim.

Set up CN IFFCO Pvt. Ltd. in collaboration with Congelados de Navarra (CN Corp) of Spain to diversify into the field of frozen vegetables.

Set up an R&D Centre at Kalol to conduct research and develop nano-fertilizers.

2019 Developed nano-nitrogen, nano-copper and nano-zinc, and launched their field trials at 11,000 locations across India. Also applied for the patent of the process for manufacturing nano-urea fertilizer.

2020 Commenced project activities for setting up a plant for producing five crore bottles of nano-urea liquid. Application was also made before the Government of India for the inclusion of nano-urea (liquid) in the Fertilizer Control Order (FCO).

2021 Nano-urea (liquid) was included in the FCO. Also, the commencement of commercial production of nano-urea at Kalol Unit.

MoU signed with two PSUs, National Fertilizers Limited and RCF for setting-up nano-urea plants based on IFFCO's technology.

Project activities for setting-up five additional plants for producing 33 crore bottles of nano-fertilizers were commenced.

2022 Production of over two crore bottles of nano-urea.

IFFCO ranked first globally according to the 11th edition of the World Cooperative Monitor 2022 Top 300 ranking released by the International Cooperative Alliance and the European Research Institute on Cooperative and Social Enterprises.

2023 IFFCO achieves the highest ever profit before tax of ₹4000 crore.

Commercial launch of IFFCO nano-DAP (liquid).

Setting up nano-urea plants at Aonla and Phulpur (Uttar Pradesh) and Deoghar (Jharkhand).

AWARDS AND RECOGNITIONS

1. Presented with the 'Eminent Chemical Engineer' award of the Indian Institute of Chemical Engineers in March 1996 by the then Vice President of India Mr Krishan Kant.
2. Chairman of the Fertilizer Association of India, New Delhi, during 1994–1996.

3. First Asian to hold the position of President of the International Fertilizer Industry Association, Paris, during 1997–1999.
4. Represented the industry point of view at the High-Level Segment in the 6th session of the United Nations Commission on Sustainable Development and delivered a speech at ECOSOC Chamber, UN Headquarters, New York, in April 1998.
5. Commitment towards Global Compact principles was appreciated by UN Secretary-General Mr Kofi A. Annan vide letter dated 12 January 2004. Awasthi was invited to attend the Global Compact Leaders' Summit held on 24 June 2004 at United Nations Headquarters in New York.
6. Honoured for cooperative development by the National Cooperative Union of India in November 1997. The Minister of Agriculture and Cooperation, Government of India, presented the citation.
7. Recipient of the Uttar Pradesh Gaurav Award presented by the Society for Environment & Agriculture Advancement in February 1996 from the then Governor of Uttar Pradesh Mr Motilal Vora.
8. Presented with the Distinguished Alumnus Award of the Society of Chemical Engineering & Technology, Banaras Hindu University, by the then Vice Chancellor Dr Hari Gautam in March 1996.
9. Recipient of the CEPM-Dr Davidson Frame Award on 11 December 2000; the award recognizes international leadership in the discipline of project management.
10. Recipient of 'Best Chief Executive of the Year 2002' from Mr Ved Prakash Goyal, Minister of Shipping, Government of India, during the Global Corporate Convention 2002 held in September 2002.
11. Conferred 'Doctor of Science (Honoria Causa)' by the Governor of Karnataka and Chancellor of University of Agricultural Sciences, Dharwad, Dr T.N. Chaturvedi, at the 20th Convocation of the University held on 25 April 2006 at Dharwad.
12. Conferred Alumni Award of Excellence 2007–2008 by Banaras Hindu University for achievements in project management and development in the fertilizer sector.
13. Was awarded IBC Leading Engineers of the World (2007) by the

International Biographical Centre, Cambridge, England.

14. Was conferred 'Doctor of Science (D.Sc.)' by the Governor of Madhya Pradesh and Chancellor of Vikram University, Ujjain, Dr Balram Jakhar, during the annual convocation of the University held on 2 March 2008 at Ujjain.

15. Was felicitated by the president of India, Smt. Pratibha Devi Singh Patil, for his outstanding contribution to the field of art and culture at Vigyan Bhawan, New Delhi, in January 2011.

16. Was conferred the 'Life Time Achievement Award' in the fertilizer sector for serving the country's farmers, cooperatives and community service by the Delhi Telugu Academy (DTA) on 30 March 2014. The award was given by the then Justice N.V. Ramana, Supreme Court of India.

17. Was felicitated by the then Vice President of India, Mr Venkaiah Naidu, with the 'Life Time Achievement Award for The Farmer, By the Farmer & To The Farmer' in the fertilizer sector constituted by DTA for serving the country's farmers, cooperatives and community service on 11 March 2018.

18. Was bestowed with the 'Late Laxman Rao Inamdar Memorial Award', on the occasion of the 6th National Convention of Sahakar Bharati organized on 22 December 2018 in Pushkar, Rajasthan, for his outstanding contribution to promoting the cooperative movement in the country. Sahakar Bharati also recognized his stupendous work in empowering farmers, ensuring food security and promoting cooperatives in India.

19. Was conferred the 'IIT (BHU) Alumnus of the Century' centenary award on February 2019 by Manoj Sinha, Minister of State, Railways, on the occasion of BHU Centenary Celebrations—Global Alumni Meet 2019 for his exceptional work throughout his career, remarkable achievements and contribution to the field of fertilizers and chemical industries.

20. Was ranked 40th in a list of '50 Most Influential Indians' for 2020 in a survey conducted by Fame India, PSU Watch and Asia Post. Dr Awasthi was the first person from the cooperative sector to have been nominated to this list.

ACKNOWLEDGEMENTS

The writing of this book was made possible by Sanjeev Ranjan, who diligently collected the material that has gone into it; Harshendra Vardhan for his contribution towards providing photographs; and Nalin Vikas, who gave a new dimension to the book. My thanks also to all of Mr Awasthi's colleagues at IFFCO and elsewhere and all those who have contributed with their memories to this book. I will be eternally grateful for their invaluable inputs.

I would also like to place on record my sincere thanks and gratitude to my editor Dibakar Ghosh of Rupa Publications for painstakingly going through the manuscript multiple times and suggesting many small and big corrections and improvements.

And most of all, I would like to thank Udai Shanker Awasthi for giving me the opportunity to present his remarkable life story to the world.

Aarnab Mitra